Julie Stafford

SOUP COOKBOOK

Julie Stafford's
SOUP
COOKBOOK

VIKING

Viking
Penguin Books Australia Ltd
487 Maroondah Highway, PO Box 257
Ringwood, Victoria 3134, Australia
Penguin Books Ltd
Harmondsworth, Middlesex, England
Penguin Putnam Inc.
375 Hudson Street, New York, New York 10014, USA
Penguin Books Canada Limited
10 Alcorn Avenue, Toronto, Ontario, Canada M4V 3B2
Penguin Books (N.Z.) Ltd
Cnr Rosedale and Airborne Roads, Albany, Auckland, New Zealand
Penguin Books (South Africa) (Pty) Ltd
5 Watkins Street, Denver Ext 4, 2094, South Africa
Penguin Books India (P) Ltd
11, Community Centre, Panchsheel Park, New Delhi 110 017, India

First published by Penguin Books Australia Ltd 2000

10 9 8 7 6 5 4 3 2 1

Design by John Canty, Penguin Design Studio
Photography by Mark Chew
Food preparation and styling by Deborah McLean
Illustrations by Michelle Katsouranis
Typeset in Garamond by Post Pre-press Group, Brisbane, Queensland
Printed and bound in Australia by Australian Print Group, Maryborough, Victoria

National Library of Australia
Cataloguing-in-Publication data:

Stafford, Julie.
 Julie Stafford's soup cookbook.

 ISBN 0 670 88666 1.

 1. Soups. I. Title.

641.813

www.penguin.com.au

Front cover photograph: Red roma tomato soup (see page 94)
with mega-grain damper (see page 122).
Back cover photograph: Minestrone (see page 79).

Contents

Introduction

Soups can be a wonderful starter and, depending on the ingredients, a substantial main meal. Many are made in just moments as meats, vegetables, pulses and herbs promptly release and marry a multitude of flavours and nutrients in a water or stock base. Soups can provide a solution to our need for fast, nutritious, cheap meals without the fuss – but with plenty of subtle, rich and intoxicating flavour.

The success of a soup begins with the stock. Indeed, some would say it is the stock that maketh the soup and other ingredients are mere passengers on the journey of flavour. Although ready-made stocks may add to the convenience of soup making, they are often loaded with ingredients that are high in saturated fat, salt, sugar and artificial flavourings. The real thing is incredibly easy and economical to make in your own kitchen. Generally the long slow cooking process releases the best flavours, so it's a good idea to make your stocks ahead of time. Stocks keep well for two to three days in the refrigerator or can easily be frozen and thawed for convenience. If you just don't have the time to make your own stocks, become a careful label reader and choose the most natural varieties available.

For a truly rich stock, use the reduction method; that is, simmer a large quantity of stock until it reduces to a small quantity. For example, allow a litre of stock to simmer away slowly until it reduces to 500 ml or 250 ml. This reduction method intensifies the flavour and increases the natural salt flavourings found in vegetables, herbs and meat bones.

Next, choose only the freshest and best ingredients to complement your stock. Look for fresh, crisp, vibrant vegetables and lush – not limp – fresh herbs. Dried herbs are best used in the cooking process and fresh herbs are best added near the very end of cooking or as a garnish when serving. Fresh herbs add lots of lovely flavours and are an excellent salt substitute. They are also rich in micronutrients. If you get the combination of ingredients right at this stage, you'll minimise the need to add traditional soup flavour-enhancers such as salt and full-fat cream.

Light-coloured stocks with subtle flavours can be made from light-coloured vegetables such as peeled onions, celery and light-green celery leaves, the white part of leeks, a few white mushroom stems, carrots, and herbs with subtle flavours like parsley. You could also add a little white wine. For darker-coloured, rich-tasting stocks try a combination of lots of mushroom trimmings and onion skins, plenty of garlic (fresh or roasted), some brown lentils, a dollop or two of tomato paste, and a dash of miso, tamari, Vecon (see page 9) or even a little red wine. However be careful not to make this stock too flavoursome or it will simply overpower the ingredients of the soup. An Asian flavour can be brought to your stock by adding ingredients such as fresh ginger, lemon grass, kaffir lime leaves, apple juice concentrate, fresh coriander and a squeeze of fresh lemon or lime juice.

Meat and chicken bones and carcasses can be added to the water with a combination of vegetables and herbs. (It's best to remove all visible fat from bones and meat before starting.) For a richer flavour, roast the bones and meat in the oven until well browned. Soup stocks made with any sort of meat bones need to be skimmed of a scum (the blood of the meat) that will appear on the top just as the stock begins to boil. Remove it with a metal spoon until the stock looks quite clear. To remove fat from a meat-based stock, allow it to stand and cool before pouring it through a very fine sieve. Stocks can be refrigerated overnight in which time any remaining fat will solidify on the top. It can then be removed easily with a metal spoon.

Old soup favourites can be revamped simply by adding a few new herbs or roasting one or two of the ingredients, or even puréeing a little of the soup for a thicker consistency. They can also be made healthier: the fat-free cooking technique (see page 12), which can be accomplished in good-quality heavy-based cookware, lets you take advantage of the natural oils in ingredients like garlic, onions and leeks rather than using butter or oil to sauté them. If it's the flavour of the oil you're after, you can always add a little when the garlic, onions and leeks are cooked.

Creamy soups needn't include full-fat cream. Try adding one or two potatoes to the soup or make one vegetable more predominant, then purée. Puréeing soups when cooked, or adding cooked barley or rice to a prepared soup and then puréeing, will also give you a creamy result. You could then add low-fat milk, soymilk or coconut milk, but be careful not to boil the soup again as boiled milk tends to curdle. Ricotta cheese thinned with a little milk will produce a pouring 'cream', while blending tofu or ricotta cheese into a cooked soup will create a thick 'cream'.

And don't forget fish soups. We've always known fish is tasty, but we now know it's also incredibly good for us. Fish has one of the highest sources of Omega 3 oils. These oils are associated with good heart health, the prevention of inflammatory diseases such as arthritis and asthma, and are essential for brain development and function. It's recommended that to obtain enough of this essential oil we should eat at least two to three meals of fish weekly. Fish soups are just another way to get the right amount of fish into your diet while you enjoy what you eat. Seafood can also be added as a garnish to pumpkin, tomato, carrot or potato soups.

Next time you need a meal in a hurry, think soup. You can turn a soup into a main meal simply by adding ingredients such as lentils, beans, chick peas, rice and fresh or dried pasta. If you serve the soup with a soup damper (see pages 118–127) or perhaps some oven-hot savoury muffins (see my *Muffin Cookbook*) you should be able to satisfy the appetites of the whole household. Use these recipes as a guideline only and enjoy experimenting with ingredients and flavours to suit your individual tastes and dietary requirements.

Good health
JULIE STAFFORD

The soup pantry

Apple juice concentrate
Apple juice concentrate is a sugar substitute with fewer kilojoules than refined sugar or honey. It's actually apple juice boiled down to make a syrup, and you'll find it at healthfood shops and supermarkets. It can be added to tomato soups to make them less acidic and to Asian-style soups to add a touch of sweetness instead of using brown sugar, sherry, wine or mirin.

Barley
Barley is a grain with a unique flavour and chewy texture. It can turn vegetable soups into main meals. Cooked barley can be added to soups and puréed to give a creamy texture.

Cheese
Parmesan is a hard Italian grating cheese with a sharp flavour. It's high in fat, so use it minimally as a garnish in soups. You only need a little to fully enjoy its flavour.

Ricotta cheese (low-fat) is a soft, creamy, white firm cheese with a bland, slightly nutty, flavour. It can be used as a cream substitute in soups. Simply blend some of the puréed soup with ricotta cheese in a food processor until smooth and of a pouring consistency. Pour this mixture back into the soup, stirring continuously, but do not bring to the boil. Or blend some ricotta cheese and milk to make a pouring 'cream' and use it to garnish a bowl of soup just as you might do with full-fat cream.

Chillies
Red chillies are generally hotter than green ones. The smaller the chilli, the hotter the taste. I mostly use red chillies, as you need only a little to get the best taste. Beware of the seeds, as this is where most of the heat lies. Remove the seeds before dicing.

Coconut milk

Coconut milk can be bought canned or powdered. It's thinner in consistency than coconut cream and much lower in fat, and it can be diluted with water or low-fat milk. To make your own coconut milk, blend ½ cup low-fat milk or soymilk with 1 tablespoon shredded coconut and strain. Coconut milk is particularly good in all laksa recipes, and a little added to soups will lend them an Asian flavour.

Cornflour

Cornflour is a fine white flour made from corn, wheat or a combination of both. It's mixed with cold water to make a paste and is used as a thickening agent. (It should always be mixed with cold liquid before adding it to a hot liquid.) Add a little to a thin soup to give it a thicker consistency or add it to soups such as spinach or broccoli as a dairy-free creamy alternative.

Herbs

A rich source of micronutrients, herbs add a burst of fresh flavour and provide an extra health dimension to a bowl of soup or a damper. To enjoy their taste and health-giving properties when at their best, herbs should be as fresh as possible. Use both the leaves and stems of fresh herbs, chopped and scattered over a soup as a garnish. I have listed some of my favourite herbs, but there are plenty of others, so explore! The amount used in each recipe is merely a guide and will vary according to your individual taste. Fresh herbs can be replaced with dried herbs (about 1 teaspoon of dried herbs is equivalent to 1 tablespoon of chopped fresh herbs), but the flavour is quite different. In soups, I prefer to add dried herbs during the cooking process and fresh herbs to garnish; in dampers, I use either fresh or dried or a combination of both.

Basil belongs to the mint family and has either green or purple foliage. It has a sweet, licorice-like flavour, and is especially good in tomato, seafood, pumpkin and vegetable soups.

Bay leaves are one of the oldest culinary herbs. When used fresh, they have a delicious sweet flavour. Add them to a stock or vegetable soup, but remember to remove them before using the stock or just before serving the soup.

Chives are one of the most popular herbs used in soups. They belong to the onion family but have a very mild taste. The fine green grass-like foliage adds a subtle onion flavour and creates an interesting texture when chopped and added to a soup as a garnish.

Coriander has delicate pale-green foliage that adds a slightly oriental, peppery flavour to soups. A little goes a long way, so use it with care. You'll mostly find it used in Asian-style soups.

Dill is a pungent, slightly sweet-tasting, herb. Its fine feathery foliage has a slightly aniseed-like taste that ideally flavours potato, celery, celeriac and tomato soups.

Garlic is one of the most popular culinary herbs. A peeled garlic clove added to a recipe imparts a very subtle garlic flavour. Chopped garlic imparts a slightly stronger garlic flavour, while crushed garlic cloves offer the most intense garlic flavour of all. One large peeled garlic clove is equivalent to ½ teaspoon crushed garlic.

Lemon grass is a lemon-scented herb resembling fine spring onions used mostly in Asian cooking.

Marjoram is very similar to oregano, though more delicate in flavour. It's perfect for both vegetable and meat soups.

Mint is recognised for its refreshing, tangy taste. It works well with split-pea soups and teams well with basil for tomato or seafood soups. Combined with coriander and chives it also tastes delicious in Asian-style soups.

Oregano is an aromatic, highly flavoured herb. Use it in soups that are typically Italian, such as rich tomato or thick vegetable and pasta soup. It's also delicious with eggplant soup.

Parsley, with its rich green colour and mild, yet distinctive, flavour, is the perfect garnish for practically any soup. It's compatible with all other herbs.

Rosemary has very fine, needle-like leaves and a strong, aromatic taste. Needless to say you need only a small amount. You can add a few sprigs or a few chopped leaves to a soup as it cooks.

Thyme is a relative of the mint family with small greenish-brown leaves. It can be used to flavour any vegetable or meat soup.

Kaffir lime leaves

Kaffir lime leaves are leaves from the kaffir lime tree used chopped or crushed in many Asian soups. You can substitute leaves from ordinary lime trees or lemon trees. Excellent as a garnish or to add an Asian flavour to chicken stock.

Mirin

Mirin is a sweet white wine used in cooking. You can substitute any white wine or a little apple juice concentrate.

Miso

Miso is a thick paste made from aged fermented soya beans and grains. You'll find it in healthfood shops and Japanese grocery stores. There are several varieties, depending on which grains are added. The dark, strong, salty miso is produced with the addition of the Japanese bean, koji. The sweet yellow miso is produced by adding rice, and the savoury red miso is the result of adding barley. (I particularly like the flavour of the dark miso. Where miso is called for in this book, I have used dark miso, although you could substitute the others and play around with flavours to suit your own tastes.) All miso varieties are rich in protein and phytochemicals. Just a little added to water produces a tasty nutritional broth for a quick pick-me-up.

Nori sheets

Nori sheets are dried sheets of seaweed used in traditional Japanese dishes such as nori rolls. They are low in fat and are a rich source of minerals such as zinc, manganese, nickel, molybdenum, selenium, copper, cobalt and chromium. You can slice them finely and add them to a thin soup just before serving.

Oils

To enjoy the flavour and health-giving benefits of vegetable and seed oils, add them to your soup after you have fat-free cooked (see page 12) ingredients such as onions, garlic, leeks and spices. When you cook these ingredients in hot oil, as in traditional cooking methods, the temperature can actually change the fatty acid structure of the oil, rendering it harmful to your health.

Olive oil is obtained by pressing the ripe pulp of the olives after picking. Its rich yellow to green colour is secondary to its fruity, flavoursome qualities. You need only a little of this oil, added to just a few soups, to enjoy its delicious fruity flavour.

Sesame seed oil is used for its strong nutty flavour and combines well with fresh ginger, garlic, chilli and apple juice concentrate, especially in Asian-style soups. You need even less than olive oil to experience its unique flavour.

Pasta

While fresh pasta cooks quickly and is ideal added to soups, the dried product made from flour (white or wholemeal) and water is just as valuable in throwing together a quick soup. Both fresh and dried pasta needs to be cooked in lots of rapidly boiling water. Keep a good supply of different types and shapes of pasta on hand. Soyaroni spiral pasta is made from soyflour and is delicious in hearty 'meal' soups. Oriental noodles are perfect for Asian-style soups. Look for hokkien noodles, shanghai noodles and soba noodles in the refrigerated section of your supermarket. There are also different types of rice noodles, both fresh and dried, that take just minutes to cook.

Pulses and lentils

Includes black beans, borlotti beans, butter beans, cannellini beans, chick peas, haricot beans, kidney beans, lentils, lima beans and soya beans. Pulses and lentils are a popular staple in the Middle East and India and are now becoming more popular in the West, particularly in vegetarian diets. They are low in fat, high in vegetable protein (especially soya beans), rich in amino acids and high in soluble fibre, which is important in controlling cholesterol. They also have a high starch content, which is digested and absorbed slowly, resulting in a slow release of glucose into the blood – ideal for controlling blood sugar levels in people with diabetes. It's necessary to thoroughly wash pulses and lentils before cooking them, and some are best soaked overnight to make them less 'gassy'. Peas and beans generally absorb about double their weight in water. When soaked, 1 cup of dried peas or beans should yield approximately 2 to 2½ cups of cooked peas or beans. It's a good idea to cook peas and beans in their soaking liquid so you don't throw valuable nutrients down the sink. You'll find many varieties of cooked pulses in cans on the supermarket shelf. Simply rinse off the liquid and you're ready to add them to a soup.

Rice
Both white and brown rice can be added to thick vegetable and meat soups. (Brown rice has three times more fibre than white rice.) Cooked rice added to a soup prior to puréeing will produce a creamy soup.

Salt
Some recipes in this book call for a pinch of salt (a small pinch is about ⅛ of a teaspoon). Salt can enhance and sharpen the flavour of many ingredients, but be careful not to overuse it. Don't use salt in every soup you make, and try using herbs and spices a little more frequently as salt substitutes. It's important to note that a high intake of salt in our diet occurs when we excessively consume canned, processed, takeaway and cured foods, which are 'hidden' sources of salt.

Sauces
Fish sauce is made from fermented anchovies and is traditionally used to flavour Thai and Vietnamese soups. Choose low-salt varieties. You can use low-salt soy sauce as a substitute.

Pesto is a sauce that traditionally combines fresh basil, pine nuts, parmesan, garlic and olive oil. It's just as flavoursome without the cheese and of course is much lower in fat. Pesto varieties are commercially available or you can make them yourself. Use as a garnish on your favourite soups or as an ingredient for a soup damper.

Soy sauce (low-salt) is a thin sauce made from fermented soya beans that adds a sharp, salty flavour to soups.

Sweet chilli sauce is a must-have condiment if you like chillies. There are different varieties available, so choose a favourite that's low in salt and sugar. You need only the tiniest amount in soup to enjoy its delicious taste, so treat yourself.

Tamari is a dark sauce made from soya beans which is similar to soy sauce, only thicker.

Soymilk

Soymilk is made from soya beans. It has similar nutritional properties to cow's milk – without the lactose, animal fats and cholesterol. It has a nutty flavour and is used in much the same way as you would use milk or cream in a soup. Low-fat and fat-free varieties are available.

Spices

Use spices in your soup recipes as an alternative to salt. As with herbs, they can make an ordinary damper an extraordinary one.

Black bean paste is a salty, fermented paste made from black beans and soya beans. It usually has added sesame oil and garlic. A typical ingredient in Chinese dishes, it produces a rich, salty flavour to your soups. Look for commercial brands made with natural ingredients.

Cayenne is a warm ground spice from the capsicum family. It adds heat to all soups and should be used sparingly.

Chilli powder is a hot, spicy powder made from the dried seeds of chilli. Like cayenne, it adds heat to soups.

Chinese five-spice powder is a pungent spice made up of cinnamon, cloves, fennel, star anise and Sichuan peppers. Use it in potato, pumpkin, tomato or carrot soups.

Cinnamon is a popular spice which comes from the bark of a tree native to Sri Lanka. Use it with other spices for curry-flavoured soups.

Cloves have a strong, sweet, unmistakable aroma, and add a warm spicy flavour to soups.

Coriander seeds are small dried seeds from the coriander plant which have been roasted. They are excellent as a garnish, or can be used with other spices such as cumin and garam masala. Delicious in potato, pumpkin, zucchini and tomato soups.

Cumin is a warm aromatic spice that teams well with coriander, garam masala and ginger in both soups and dampers.

Curry paste should be used sparingly in soup recipes and has a more intense flavour than curry powder (1 teaspoon of curry paste can be substituted for 1 tablespoon of curry powder). Of the prepared curry pastes available I particularly like a hot vindaloo variety and a milder red curry paste.

Curry powder is a blend of spices usually comprised of varying amounts of the following ground herbs and spices: coriander, turmeric, chilli, cumin, fennel, fenugreek, mustard, ginger, cinnamon, nutmeg and cloves.

Garam masala is a fragrant Indian blend of cardamom, cinnamon, coriander, cumin, fenugreek, ginger, pepper and turmeric. It adds warmth and aroma to soups.

Ginger is an interesting-looking knobbly root. Look for young ginger with taught, thin skin as they are less fibrous and more juicy. Remove the skin and finely dice or place small pieces in a garlic press. Ginger is prized for its sweet, yet slightly spicy, flavour. It also aids and enhances digestion.

Ginger (ground) is mildly spicy and warm and is often teamed with other spices such as garam masala, garlic powder, cumin and cardamom in curry-style soups.

Nutmeg is better when used fresh and grated to capture its sweet, nutty flavour. It's ideal as a soup garnish.

Pepper, black (ground) is a rather sharp, hot spice. For a more subtle pepper flavour, use white pepper.

Sambal oelek is a very hot south-east Asian condiment or accompaniment made from red chillies.

Turmeric belongs to the ginger family. It's a bright yellow–orange spice that has a mild, slightly peppery taste.

Tomato paste

Tomato paste is a concentrated purée of tomatoes. It adds a depth of colour and rich tomato flavour to soup. Look for salt-free or low-salt commercial varieties, or make your own tomato paste by peeling and seeding the tomatoes, chopping them finely, and cooking them until they reduce and thicken.

Tofu

Tofu is a bland-tasting unfermented soya bean curd. It's made by adding a natural coagulant such as lemon juice to soymilk in order to create curds. The excess milk is drained off and the curds are pressed into blocks to further remove all liquid. Tofu is an excellent source of protein, is rich in natural phytoestrogens and calcium, and is both low in fat and cholesterol free. It's available in a firm form, which can be grilled and added to laksas, or a soft silken form. Tofu can be blended into soups to make them thick and creamy.

Vecon

Look for Vecon at your local healthfood shop or in the health section of your supermarket. It's a thick, dark, concentrated vegetable paste, sold in small 225 g glass jars. It's loaded with the combined concentrated flavours of onion, celery, tomato, carrot, parsley, garlic, paprika, spinach, beetroot, celery seed, horseradish, yeast extract and seaweed, and it's particularly high in the B-group vitamins B1, B2 and B12.

Yoghurt

Low-fat yoghurt is a cultured milk product. Specific bacteria are added to warm, fresh low-fat (cow's, goat's or sheep's) milk to develop a tangy custard-like yoghurt. It's more nutritious than milk because an extra 4 per cent of fat-free milk powder is added to enhance the texture. Yoghurt contains *lactobacillus acidophilus*, a healthy bacteria that is thought to help rectify imbalances of healthy organisms in the gut. During the yoghurt-making process, fat and protein in the yoghurt are broken down, turning lactose into lactic acid, which makes it easily digestible. Look for varieties that have a fat content of approximately 0.1 per cent. Yoghurt can be used in much the same way as milk or cream in soup or damper recipes. It's especially good as a garnish for curried soups.

Glossary of cooking terms

Al dente
A term generally used for cooking pasta and rice but also used for vegetables. It means to cook a food until just tender, yet still retaining a little bite.

Blanch
To plunge raw food in boiling water, then in cold.

Vegetables Blanching enhances colour, removes bitter tastes and loosens the skins of some vegetables. Place raw vegetables in boiling water, leave for just a few minutes depending on size, and remove. Immediately refresh by plunging into iced water for a few minutes to cool completely. Use as recipe suggests. Alternatively vegetables can be steam-blanched in the microwave.

Meat bones Blanching meat bones helps to reduce the amount of scum that forms in meat-based stocks and soups. Place meat bones in boiling water, leave for just a few minutes then remove. Immediately run under cold water to remove scum. Meat-based stocks and soups will still need to be skimmed of scum, which rises to the top in the cooking process.

Seafood An ideal method of cooking scallops, calamari and prawns. Quickly plunge them in a little simmering stock or white wine until they change colour.

Bruise
A term that describes the partial crushing of foods like garlic, ginger, lemon grass or peppercorns. Bruising can be done between the fingers, with the handle of a large knife or in a mortar and pestle.

Chargrill
To cook vegetables, meat and seafood over a hot grill pan that is specially designed for chargrilling. The hot grill gives the cooked food distinctive scorch lines and a wood-fired, smoky flavour. If the pan is

very hot before you place food on it, there should be no need to add any oil. The very hot surface will seal the food quickly, allowing no juices to escape.

Chop
To cut food roughly into no particular shape or size.

Degorge
This is a simple process of removing the bitter juices from an eggplant prior to cooking. (It's not necessary to use this process with young eggplant as the bitter juices have not yet developed.) Cut eggplant as recipe suggests. Place in a bowl and add salt liberally. Cover and allow eggplant to stand for at least 2 hours. Rinse eggplant under cold running water to remove salt and bitter juices. Dry eggplant well before cooking.

Dice
The process of chopping food into very small even cubes.

Dry-roast
To cook food in a hot oven, allowing the dry heat to seal in the food juices. The heat is then turned down and cooked slowly, allowing roasting flavours to intensify.

Fat-free cook
Often we use fat in the cooking process just so food doesn't stick to the pan. A little water, stock, fruit juice or wine can be used instead of fats and oils to cook food in its initial stages. Food will cook and brown naturally without the need to add any fat or oils. A browning effect can be achieved by cooking foods in heavy-based cookware. Simply place food like onions, leeks, garlic and ginger into a cold, dry, heavy-based pan and cover with a lid. Heat and allow food to cook slowly in its own natural oils or juices. For cookware that does not have a heavy base, wipe the surface of the pan with just a little cooking oil and don't cook the food at excessively high temperatures.

Julienne
To cut vegetables (for example, zucchini and carrots) into very thin matchstick strips.

Pinch
The small amount of salt, pepper, dried herbs or spices that can be held between two fingertips.

Poach
To cook foods in simmering liquid (for example, water, wine, stock or juice).

Purée
To blend food to a smooth texture in a blender or food processor.

Roast
For stock making, roasting simply means to place meat bones or vegetables in a pan with some chopped onions and a little olive oil (or other ingredients as recipe suggests), cover and bake in a moderately hot oven until well browned. Drain off oil before adding to a large soup pot with other stock ingredients.

Sauté
To cook food in a little oil until it softens and browns.

Simmer
To cook food in a hot liquid which is just bubbling.

Steam cook
To place food on a rack or specially designed steamer above boiling liquid, where the steam – not the water – penetrates and cooks the food. Food can also be steam-cooked in a microwave oven.

STOCKS

The success of a soup begins with the stock. Indeed, some would say it is the stock that maketh the soup and other ingredients are mere passengers on the journey of flavour.

Chicken stocks

A whole chicken, chicken bones, carcasses, neck and wings are all suitable. Chicken stock is one of the most popular and flavoursome stocks used to make a variety of soups. Chicken bones and carcasses are quite gelatinous. If allowed to set they produce a jelly-like stock which provides a rich, velvety texture to all soups made with it.

Basic chicken stock
Makes 1–2 litres

1.5–2 kg whole chicken or chicken bones, carcass, wings or neck

2 onions (skins on), chopped

2 sticks celery (with leaves), chopped

2 carrots, chopped

8–12 black peppercorns

few sprigs of parsley

5 litres water

1 cup white wine

- If using whole chicken, tie legs together and place in a deep soup pot. Add all other ingredients and bring to the boil. Remove scum as it rises. Reduce heat and simmer for 1½ hrs or until chicken is cooked and tender. Remove chicken and set aside.

- Simmer for another hour. Strain through a fine sieve and discard vegetable matter.

- When completely cooled, remove any fat that has risen to the surface before using.

This stock is delicious just as it is and can be served as a light lunch broth. Simply add some finely chopped vegetables such as carrot, celery, spinach and spring onions and your favourite finely chopped fresh herbs.

Asian chicken stock
Makes 1–2 litres

1.5–2 kg chicken bones, carcass, wings or neck	2 stalks lemon grass (white part only)
2 onions (skins on), chopped	2 star anise
2 cloves garlic, peeled	3 kaffir lime leaves
1 x 2-cm piece fresh ginger, peeled	few sprigs of fresh coriander (with root)
2 sticks celery (with leaves), chopped	5 litres water
	1 cup white wine

- Place chicken bones in a large soup pot. Add all other ingredients and bring to the boil. Remove scum as it rises. Reduce heat and simmer for 1 hour.

- Strain through a fine sieve and discard vegetable and spice matter.

- When completely cooled, remove any fat that has risen to the surface before using.

This stock is delicious just as it is and can be served as a light lunch broth. To sweeten, add a little apple juice concentrate, mirin or sherry. Then add some finely chopped vegetables such as carrot, red capsicum, bok choy, bean sprouts, spring onions and finely chopped fresh coriander and mint. For a more hearty soup, add some chunks of grilled tofu.

Roasted chicken stock
Makes 1–2 litres

1.5–2 kg whole chicken

2 onions (skins on), chopped

1 leek, thoroughly washed and chopped

2 carrots, chopped

2 sticks celery (with leaves), chopped

8–12 black peppercorns

3–4 bay leaves

6 litres water

- Tie chicken legs together. In a heavy-based pan, fat-free cook (see page 12) chicken until brown on all sides. Remove chicken from pan. Add onions, leek and carrots to the pan and continue to fat-free cook them until soft and beginning to brown. Allow them to become quite brown, but don't allow them to burn.

- Place browned chicken, onions, leek and carrots in a large soup pot. Add all other ingredients and bring to the boil. Remove scum as it rises. Reduce heat and simmer for 1 to 1½ hours or until chicken is cooked and tender. Remove chicken and set aside. (Chicken meat can be chopped and added to soup just prior to serving. It's best to cover chicken to stop it from drying out.)

- Simmer for another hour. Strain through a fine sieve and discard vegetable matter.

- When completely cooled, remove any fat that has risen to the surface before using.

This stock is darker and richer than basic chicken stock. It's delicious just as it is and can be served as a light lunch broth. Simply add some finely chopped vegetables such as carrot, celery, spinach and spring onions and your favourite finely chopped fresh herbs.

Fish stocks

Use only the bones and trimmings of the freshest white fish and simmer for no more than 30 minutes. Overcooked fish stock can be rather bitter and spoil the taste of the soup. Fish bones release their flavour quickly, so it's a good idea to chop any added vegetables finely so they too can rapidly release their flavours.

Basic fish stock
Makes 1 litre

1 kg fish bones and trimmings (heads, tails and skin)	1 stick celery, finely chopped
	½ small lemon
1 leek (white part only), thoroughly washed and finely chopped	4–6 black peppercorns
	2 litres water
50 g mushroom trimmings (peel and stems), cleaned	

- Place all ingredients in a large soup pot and simmer uncovered for 30 minutes. Allow stock to cool before straining through a fine sieve. Discard bones and vegetable matter.

- Further simmer stock to reduce or add extra water, white wine or chicken stock to make up the required amount.

This stock can be refrigerated for up to 2 days or frozen and used as required.

Fragrant fish stock
Makes 1 litre

1 kg fish bones and trimmings (heads, tails and skin)

1 onion, peeled and finely chopped

rind of an orange, chopped

2 bay leaves

few sprigs of fresh basil

few sprigs of fresh fennel

sprig of fresh thyme

1 cup white wine

10 pink peppercorns

2 litres water

- Place all ingredients in a large soup pot and simmer uncovered for 30 minutes. Allow stock to cool before straining through a fine sieve. Discard bones and vegetable matter.

- Further simmer stock to reduce or add extra water, white wine or chicken stock to make up the required amount.

This stock can be refrigerated for up to 2 days or frozen and used as required.

Meat stocks

Bones and carcasses produce the best flavour, but chunks of fresh or roasted meat can also be used. Meat stocks need to be cooked longer than fish or vegetable stocks, as meat bones release their delicious flavours more slowly.

Fresh meat bones and carcasses can be blanched (see page 11) before adding them to other stock ingredients. This process helps to remove much of the blood and reduces the amount of scum that inevitably forms in meat-based stocks and soups. They can also be roasted (see page 13) for a richer flavoured, darker coloured stock.

Fresh meat bones can be stored in a plastic bag or container in the freezer. Alternatively your local butcher would be delighted to sell you a couple of kilos of beef, chicken or lamb bones. All meat-based stocks need to be completely cooled and have all visible fat removed before using.

Beef stock
Makes 1–2 litres

2 kg beef bones, blanched or roasted	2 bay leaves
2 carrots, chopped	few sprigs of parsley
2 onions (skins on), chopped	sprig of fresh thyme
2 cups chopped green celery leaves	12 black peppercorns
	6 litres water

- Place all ingredients in a large soup pot and simmer uncovered for 4 to 6 hours. Remove scum as it rises until stock is quite clear. Allow stock to cool before straining through a fine sieve. Discard bones and vegetable matter.

- Further simmer stock to reduce to approximately 1 to 2 litres.

- When completely cooled, remove any fat that has risen to the surface before using.

Lamb shank stock
Makes 1–2 litres

1 kg lamb shanks (all visible fat removed), blanched or roasted

2 onions (skins on), chopped

1 leek, thoroughly washed and chopped

1 cup chopped celery leaves

2 carrots, chopped

8–12 black peppercorns

few sprigs of parsley

6 litres water

½ cup barley

- Place all ingredients except barley in a large soup pot. Cover and simmer for 2 to 3 hours or until shank meat is cooked and tender. Remove scum as it rises until stock is quite clear. Remove shanks, cover and allow to cool. (The meat can be chopped and added to soup just prior to serving.)

- Strain through a fine sieve and discard vegetable matter. Return stock to a cleaned soup pot and add barley. Simmer uncovered for a further 2 hours or until barley is soft and stock has reduced to 1 or 2 litres. Strain soup as before and discard barley.

- When completely cooled, remove any fat that has risen to the surface before using.

This stock is delicious just as it is and can be served as a light lunch broth. Simply add some of your favourite finely chopped fresh herbs.

Miso stock

A staple ingredient in a Japanese diet and popular in vegetarian and macrobiotic diets, miso can be made up in larger quantities and used as a stock for fish soups, thick vegetable and bean soups, and creamy smooth vegetable soups. As it is high in sodium, it should be used in moderation on a low-salt diet. The paste is best dissolved in boiling water before adding it to larger quantities of liquid. For a broth-style soup, it is best simmered rather than boiled, as boiling tends to make it separate. Because it has already gone through a fermentation process, miso will keep indefinitely in the refrigerator in a sealed container.

Makes 1 litre

¼–½ cup miso paste   1 litre boiling water

• Dissolve miso paste in boiling water.

Vecon stock

Vecon can be found at your local healthfood shop or in the health section of your supermarket. It's best dissolved in boiling water before adding it to larger quantities of liquid. When you haven't got time to make your own stock, this is an ideal alternative.

Makes 1 litre

1 tablespoon Vecon paste   3½ cups water
½ cup boiling water

• Dissolve Vecon paste in boiling water then add cold water.

Vegetable stocks

Use clean vegetable peelings or whole vegetables. Vegetable stock should not be overcooked or it will taste a little stewed. Avoid adding strong-flavoured vegetables such as broccoli, brussels sprouts, cabbage, corn and cauliflower to stock: these are best added to a soup when it's nearly cooked.

Dark roasted vegetable stock
Makes 2 litres

4 brown onions (skins on), chopped

2 carrots, chopped

2 parsnips, chopped

2–4 sticks celery, chopped

4 cloves garlic, peeled

2 tablespoons olive oil

freshly ground black pepper

sprig of fresh rosemary

2 teaspoons miso or Vecon dissolved in ¼ cup boiling water

2 tablespoons tomato paste (optional)

few sprigs of parsley

4–6 litres water

- Place first 7 ingredients in a shallow baking tray, toss well, and bake in a moderately hot oven until vegetables are cooked and well browned. (The darker the vegetables, the darker the stock; but be careful not to burn them.) Drain off fat.

- Place the vegetables along with all other ingredients in a large soup pot and simmer uncovered for 1½ to 2 hours. Allow stock to cool before straining through a fine sieve. Discard vegetable matter.

- Further simmer stock to reduce to approximately 2 litres.

- When completely cooled, remove any fat that has risen to the surface before using.

Dark vegetable stock
Makes 2 litres

2 brown onions (skins on), chopped

2 carrots, chopped

2–4 sticks celery, chopped

100 g mushroom trimmings (peel and stems)

1 tablespoon miso or Vecon dissolved in ¼ cup boiling water

2 tablespoons tomato paste

4–6 cloves garlic, roasted

few sprigs of parsley

8–12 black peppercorns

4–6 litres water

Optional

extra brown onion skins

1–2 tablespoons low-salt soy sauce

1 leek (green part only), chopped

1 green capsicum, seeded and chopped

½ cup brown lentils

½ cup pearl barley

- Place all ingredients in a large soup pot and simmer uncovered for 1½ hours. Allow stock to cool before straining through a fine sieve. Discard vegetable matter.

- Further simmer stock to reduce to approximately 2 litres.

Note Only add lentils or pearl barley to stock that is already boiling.

Light vegetable stock
Makes 2 litres

2 onions, peeled and chopped

2 carrots, chopped

2–4 sticks celery, chopped

2 zucchini, chopped

2 bay leaves

few sprigs of parsley

8–12 black peppercorns

4–6 litres water

Optional

2 parsnips, chopped

1 leek (white part only),
thoroughly washed and chopped

few sprigs of fresh thyme,
marjoram or dill

fresh ginger, peeled

garlic cloves, peeled

- In a heavy-based pan, fat-free cook (see page 12) onion, leek, garlic and ginger until soft and beginning to brown. Add these and all other ingredients to a large soup pot and simmer uncovered for 1½ hours. Allow stock to cool before straining through a fine sieve. Discard vegetable matter.

- Further simmer stock to reduce to approximately 2 litres.

SOUPS

Soups can provide a solution to our need for fast, nutritious,
cheap meals without the fuss — but with plenty of subtle,
rich and intoxicating flavour.

Asian asparagus soup

An easy summer soup that takes no time at all to prepare as it uses a good-quality prepared curry paste with typical Asian flavours.

1 onion, peeled and diced

3 teaspoons green curry paste

800 g fresh asparagus spears

200 g potato, peeled and chopped

1 litre Asian chicken stock (page 17), basic chicken stock (page 16) or light vegetable stock (page 26)

finely chopped fresh coriander to garnish

- In a heavy-based pan, fat-free cook (see page 12) onion and curry paste until onion begins to soften.

- Add asparagus, potato and stock. Bring to the boil, cover and simmer for 15 to 20 minutes or until asparagus and potato are just tender. Purée soup.

- Serve garnished with coriander.

Asparagus, spinach and tofu soup

Serves 4–6

This soup is rich in phytoestrogens and full of flavour.

1 litre basic chicken stock (page 16) or miso stock (page 23)

1 onion, peeled and finely diced

1 stick celery, thinly sliced

2 cloves garlic

2 bay leaves

2 sprigs tarragon

200 g fresh asparagus, thinly diagonally sliced

200 g spinach leaves, washed and torn into pieces

400 g silken tofu, cut into cubes

freshly ground black pepper

finely chopped fresh coriander or chervil to garnish

- Place stock, onion, celery, garlic, bay leaves and tarragon in a large soup pot. Bring to the boil, cover and simmer for 20 minutes.

- Remove garlic, bay leaves and tarragon and discard.

- Add asparagus and cook until it is just tender and a vibrant green. Then add spinach and continue cooking until it just wilts. Add tofu to warm through.

- Add pepper to taste.

- Serve garnished with coriander or chervil.

Avocado soup

Serves 4–6

This soup is best served chilled. It's ideal for a light lunch or served before a warm curry meal.

300 g celery

300 g carrots

2 teaspoons crushed garlic

flesh of 2 ripe avocados

squeeze of fresh lemon juice

1 cup low-fat yoghurt or 200 g silken low-fat tofu

pinch cayenne pepper

¼ cup finely chopped fresh chives

- Thoroughly wash celery and carrots and juice in a fruit and vegetable juicer. Discard fibrous pulp.

- Place celery and carrot juice, garlic, avocado, lemon juice and yoghurt or tofu in a food processor and blend until smooth.

- Add cayenne pepper to taste.

- Stir through the chives and serve.

Basilica tomato and mussel soup

Serves 4–6

Before you begin, find a fishmonger who will sell you only the freshest and best mussels – anything less is not acceptable.

40 mussels

1 onion, peeled and diced

1 teaspoon crushed garlic

2 x 425 g cans salt-free tomatoes and juice

1 x 140 g tub tomato paste

½ teaspoon basil

½ teaspoon oregano

1 cup white wine

2 cups basic fish stock (page 19) or basic chicken stock (page 16)

10 fresh basil leaves, finely chopped

extra fresh basil leaves to garnish

- Wash the mussels thoroughly and remove the beard.

- Place onion, garlic, tomatoes, tomato paste, basil and oregano in a food processor and blend until smooth.

- Pour into a heavy-based pan along with the wine. Bring to the boil, cover and simmer for 10 minutes.

- Add stock and basil. Cover and simmer a further 20 minutes.

- Add mussels. Cover and simmer for just a few minutes or until mussels open. (Have some extra stock or wine on hand in case the soup is too thick.)

- Serve immediately, garnished with basil leaves.

Bean-a-lot soup

Serves 6–8

A thick, rich and hearty soup with lots of healthy beans.

1 onion, peeled and chopped

2 teaspoons crushed garlic

2 teaspoons finely chopped fresh ginger

2 teaspoons cumin

1 teaspoon paprika

1 teaspoon coriander

1 litre miso stock (page 23), beef stock (page 21) or dark vegetable stock (page 25)

1 cup red wine

1 x 140 g tub tomato paste

1 x 425 g can salt-free tomatoes and juice, puréed

1 carrot, diced

1 zucchini, sliced

1 red pepper, seeded and diced

1 yellow pepper, seeded and diced

1 x 750 g can Four Bean Mix, well drained

finely chopped spring onions to garnish

- In a heavy-based pan, fat-free cook (see page 12) onion, garlic, ginger and spices until onion begins to soften and brown.

- Add all other ingredients except beans. Bring to the boil, cover and simmer for 20 to 30 minutes or until vegetables are tender.

- Add beans and stir well. Cook a further 5 to 10 minutes or until beans are heated through.

- Serve garnished with spring onions.

Note Have some extra stock on hand in case the soup is too thick. If you allow the soup to cool before serving, the beans will swell and absorb a lot of the stock.

Beef, noodle and greens soup

Serves 4–6

Prepare a rich-flavoured stock and you'll always be rewarded with a prize-winning soup.

400 g lean eye fillet, thinly sliced

1 onion, peeled and sliced

2 teaspoons crushed garlic

2 teaspoons finely chopped fresh ginger

1 litre beef stock (page 21), miso stock (page 23) or dark vegetable stock (page 25), boiling

2 tablespoons dry sherry

2 tablespoons low-salt soy sauce

400 g fresh noodles (rice, hokkien, shanghai or soba)

100 g spinach, chopped

100 g bean shoots

4 spring onions, thinly sliced

freshly ground black pepper

- In a heavy-based pan, fat-free cook (see page 12) beef, onion, garlic and ginger until the meat is brown on both sides, but still very tender.

- Add all other ingredients except spinach, bean shoots, spring onions and pepper. Stirring continuously, simmer for 3 to 5 minutes or until noodles are heated through.

- Add spinach, bean shoots and spring onions and cook a further minute or until just heated through.

- Add pepper to taste and serve.

Black-eyed bean and vegetable soup

Serves 6–8

If you're introducing beans into your diet for the first time, black-eyed beans are an excellent choice. You can't miss these little kidney-shaped beans: they have a distinctive black eye. Like other beans they are low in fat and high in protein and fibre, yet unlike their counterparts they tend to be sweeter in flavour. Overnight soaking produces the best results. You can chop and change the vegetables depending on what you like or what's in season.

1 cup dry black-eyed beans	½ teaspoon oregano
3 cups cold water	½ teaspoon mint
1 onion, peeled and thinly sliced	½ teaspoon celery seed
200 g carrots, cut into thin rounds	½ teaspoon coriander
2 sticks celery, thinly sliced	freshly ground black pepper
1 red capsicum, seeded and chopped	2 litres basic chicken stock (page 16)
200 g sweet potato, peeled	1 tablespoon fish sauce
1 teaspoon basil	finely chopped fresh herbs (dill, basil, chives) to garnish
1 teaspoon cumin	

- Cover beans with cold water and soak overnight. Discard any broken beans before soaking as well as those that rise to the top during soaking. They will double in size so you'll end up with 2 cups of swollen beans. Drain well.

- Combine all ingredients except herbs (for garnish) in a large soup pot. Bring to the boil, cover and simmer for 2 hours.

- Serve garnished with herbs.

Broccoli and spinach soup

Serves 4–6

You'll find cardamom in many Indian recipes. Similar to cloves, it is spicy, yet sweet and aromatic, and it blends beautifully with the warmth of nutmeg.

250 g broccoli	¼ teaspoon cardamom
250 g spinach leaves	¼ teaspoon nutmeg
2 leeks, thoroughly washed and chopped	1 litre basic chicken stock (page 16) or miso stock (page 23)
1 tablespoon crushed garlic	low-fat yoghurt to garnish
1 tablespoon tomato paste	extra nutmeg to garnish

- Steam cook (see page 13) broccoli and spinach until just tender and a vibrant green.

- In a heavy-based pan, fat-free cook (see page 12) leeks and garlic until leeks begin to soften and brown.

- Add tomato paste, cardomom, nutmeg and stock. Simmer for 10 minutes.

- Add broccoli and spinach and heat through. Purée soup.

- Serve garnished with yoghurt and nutmeg.

Brown lentil soup

Serves 4–6

This is the sort of soup you might find on the menu of a Greek tavern. Rich in vegetable protein and essential amino acids, it's incredibly easy to make and it tastes incredibly good.

2 onions, peeled and chopped

1 x 375 g packet brown lentils

2 litres beef stock (page 21) or miso stock (page 23)

2 cups water

1 x 140 g tub tomato paste

1 tablespoon tamari

2 sprigs fresh rosemary

freshly ground black pepper

squeeze of fresh lemon juice

finely chopped parsley to garnish

- Combine all ingredients except pepper, lemon juice and parsley in a large soup pot. Bring to the boil, cover and simmer for 1 hour or until lentils are soft and soup is thick. Discard rosemary. Purée a little of the soup (this helps to thicken the soup) and return it to the pot.

- Add pepper and lemon juice to taste.

- Serve garnished with parsley.

Cabbage and vegetable soup

Serves 4–6

You would probably find this soup on the menu at an English or Irish corner pub.

1.5 litres beef stock (page 21) or miso stock (page 23)

1 leek, thoroughly washed and thinly sliced

1½ teaspoons tarragon

½ teaspoon thyme

2 sticks celery, chopped

3 carrots, chopped

2 parsnips, chopped

¼ cup brown rice or 200 g potato, peeled and chopped

½ small white cabbage, roughly chopped

grated parmesan cheese to garnish

finely chopped fresh parsley to garnish

- Combine all ingredients except cabbage, cheese and parsley in a large soup pot. Bring to the boil, cover and simmer for 1 hour or until rice and vegetables are well cooked. Stir occasionally to prevent rice sticking to the base of pot.

- Add cabbage and cook a further 20 minutes. Purée a little of the soup (this helps to thicken the soup) and return it to the pot.

- Serve garnished with cheese and parsley.

Carrot and roasted parsnip soup

Serves 4–6

Although one is bright orange and the other a creamy white, these two vegetables are from the same family. Both are sweet-tasting, with the parsnip flavour being uniquely nutty.

400 g parsnip

2 onions, peeled and diced

600 g carrots, chopped

1 litre light vegetable stock (page 26), basic chicken stock (page 16) or roasted chicken stock (page 18)

2 cups low-fat milk or low-fat soymilk

nutmeg to garnish

- Preheat oven to 200°C.

- Cut parsnip in half longways and place on an oven tray lined with non-stick baking paper. Dry-roast (see page 12) the parsnips for 30 to 40 minutes or until soft in the centre and brown on the outside. Remove from oven, cool and roughly chop.

- Combine onions, carrots and stock in a large soup pot. Bring to the boil, cover and simmer for 20 to 30 minutes or until carrots are soft.

- Add parsnips and purée the soup until thick and creamy. Add milk and reheat, but do not boil.

- Serve garnished with nutmeg.

Opposite: Curried scallop and sweet potato soup (see page 63) with corn and cumin damper (see page 120).

Carrot and walnut soup

Serves 4–6

Sweet with the warm woody flavour of walnuts . . .

1 onion, peeled and chopped

800 g sweet young carrots, chopped

200 g potatoes, peeled and chopped

1 teaspoon finely chopped fresh ginger

½ teaspoon cumin

2 teaspoons finely grated orange zest

1 litre light vegetable stock (page 26), beef stock (page 21) or basic chicken stock (page 16)

20 walnuts, dry-roasted

finely chopped chives to garnish

- Place all ingredients except walnuts and chives in a large soup pot. Bring to the boil, cover and simmer until vegetables are soft.

- Remove the soup from heat and purée until smooth and creamy.

- Stir in the walnuts.

- Serve garnished with chives.

Opposite: Green pea, basil and mint soup (see page 72) with sun-dried tomato, olive and onion damper (see page 127).

Cauliflower, coconut and coriander soup

Serves 4–6

You'd swear this soup was full of cream, but it's not. If you can't afford the airfare to Thailand, then this soup is the next best thing!

800 g cauliflower, chopped

300 g potatoes, peeled and chopped

400 g leek (white part only), thoroughly washed and chopped

1 teaspoon cumin

½ teaspoon coriander

3 cups light vegetable stock (page 26) or basic chicken stock (page 16)

400 ml coconut milk

2 tablespoons finely chopped fresh coriander

1–2 tablespoons finely grated lemon or lime rind

- Place all ingredients except coconut milk, coriander and lemon or lime rind in a large soup pot. Bring to the boil, cover and simmer until cauliflower and potatoes are just tender. It's important not to overcook the vegetables: overcooked cauliflower does not taste particularly pleasant.

- Remove the soup from heat and purée until smooth.

- Stir in the coconut milk. Return soup to heat through, but do not boil.

- Stir through the coriander and lemon or lime rind, and serve.

Celery and potato soup

Serves 4–6

Have you ever wondered what to do with the celery leaves from a bunch of celery? This economical and tasty soup recipe provides the perfect answer.

3 onions, peeled and chopped

300 g celery leaves, thoroughly washed

4 cloves garlic, peeled

1 kg potatoes, peeled and chopped

1 litre light vegetable stock (page 26) or basic chicken stock (page 16)

2 teaspoons dill

freshly ground black pepper

finely chopped fresh herbs (dill, parsley, chives) to garnish

- In a heavy-based pan, fat-free cook (see page 12) onions, celery and garlic until onions and celery begin to soften.

- Add potatoes, stock and dill. Bring to the boil, cover and simmer for 20 to 30 minutes or until potato is tender. Purée soup.

- Add pepper to taste.

- Serve garnished with herbs.

Chicken laksa

Laksa is a fragrant and spicy noodle-based dish served in a soup. You can buy a commercial laksa paste or substitute a red curry paste when you're in a hurry, but nothing tastes quite like the combination of fresh ingredients you can mix together in your own kitchen. The ingredients are all readily available at fresh food markets and most good grocery shops. Laksa paste ingredients can be chopped very finely or ground to a smooth paste in a food processor.

boiling water

200 g rice noodles

200 g snow peas, thinly sliced

100 g zucchini, cut into julienne strips

600 g chicken fillet (skin and fat removed), cut into bite-sized pieces

1 litre basic chicken stock (page 16), boiling

140 ml coconut milk

100 g bean shoots

fresh coriander to garnish

Laksa paste

1 teaspoon sesame oil

1 onion, peeled and finely diced

3 cloves garlic, peeled and crushed

3 teaspoons finely chopped fresh ginger

1 tablespoon finely chopped fresh lemon grass (approx. 1 stem, white part only)

6 macadamia nuts, finely chopped

1 teaspoon turmeric

1 teaspoon cumin

½ teaspoon ground coriander

2 teaspoons sweet chilli sauce

1 tablespoon fish sauce

2 tablespoons apple juice concentrate

- Pour boiling water over noodles in a large bowl and allow them to soak for 2 to 3 minutes or until soft. Drain well.

- Blanch (see page 11) snow peas and zucchini.

- In a heavy-based pan, cook the first 9 ingredients of the laksa paste until onion softens and spices are fragrant. Add remaining ingredients and cook for a further minute, stirring continuously.

- Add chicken and coat well with laksa paste.

- Add boiling chicken stock. Simmer for approximately 5 minutes or until chicken is just cooked and tender.

- Stir in the coconut milk and heat through, but do not boil.

- Place equal amounts of cooked noodles at the bottom of each soup bowl. Add snow peas and zucchini and top with bean shoots.

- Ladle spoonfuls of soup over the noodles and vegetables.

- Serve garnished with coriander.

Chicken minestrone with pesto

Serves 8

This makes for a pleasant change from traditional minestrone. I've included a recipe for both red and green pesto. I like both as a garnish with this soup – try both and decide which one you like best.

1 cup dried red kidney beans

2 teaspoons crushed garlic

2 onions, peeled and chopped

2 sticks celery, thinly sliced

2.5 litres basic chicken stock (page 16) or roasted chicken stock (page 18)

¼ cup salt-free tomato paste

2 teaspoons basil

1 teaspoon oregano

½ teaspoon thyme

½ cup risoni pasta

1 x 425 g can salt-free tomatoes and juice

2 large carrots, cut into rounds

20 French beans, topped and tailed and cut into four pieces each

extra chicken stock (optional)

2 cups finely shredded cabbage

400 g cooked chicken (remove skin and fat before cooking)

freshly ground black pepper

green or red pesto to garnish

- Cover beans with cold water and soak overnight. Discard any broken beans before soaking as well as those that rise to the top during soaking. Drain well.

- Place beans and the first 9 ingredients in a large soup pot. Bring to the boil, cover and simmer for approximately 2 hours.

- Add risoni and cook for a further 20 minutes. Stir occasionally to prevent beans and pasta sticking to the base of pot.

- Add tomatoes, carrots and beans and cook until vegetables are tender. Check consistency of soup at this stage and add a little extra stock if soup is too thick.

- Add cabbage and cook a further 15 minutes or until cabbage is quite tender.

- Add cooked chicken and heat through.

- Add black pepper to taste.

- Serve garnished with green or red pesto.

Green pesto (Makes ¼ cup)

50 g fresh basil leaves, stems removed	1 tablespoon grated parmesan cheese (optional)
½ cup pine nuts	pinch salt
1–2 teaspoons crushed garlic	pinch finely ground black pepper
1 tablespoon olive oil	

- Combine basil, pine nuts and garlic in a food processor and process until smooth. While food processor is still operating, drizzle in the oil and cheese.

- Add salt and pepper to taste.

Red pesto (Makes ½ cup)

1–2 red capsicums, seeded, chargrilled and chopped	1 tablespoon olive oil
100 g fresh basil leaves, stems removed	1–2 tablespoons grated parmesan cheese (optional)
½ cup pine nuts	pinch salt
1–2 teaspoons crushed garlic	pinch finely ground black pepper

- Combine capsicums, basil, pine nuts and garlic in a food processor and process until smooth. While food processor is still operating, drizzle in the oil and cheese.

- Add salt and pepper to taste.

Chicken noodle soup

Serves 6–8

If your children love 'worms' in their soup, they'll love this recipe. Big children love it too!

4 onions, peeled and thinly sliced

2 teaspoons crushed garlic

600 g chicken fillet (skin and fat removed), cut into bite-sized pieces

½ teaspoon turmeric

2 sticks celery, thinly sliced

2 carrots, grated

2 litres basic chicken stock (page 16)

100 g angel hair pasta

freshly ground black pepper

finely chopped fresh parsley to garnish

- In a heavy-based pan, fat-free cook (see page 12) onions, garlic, chicken and turmeric until onion is soft and chicken begins to brown. Remove ingredients from pan, cover and keep warm.

- Add vegetables and stock, cover and bring to the boil. Add pasta and stir well. Simmer, stirring occasionally, for 15 to 20 minutes or until vegetables are soft and pasta is al dente.

- Return the cooked chicken and onion to the pan and simmer gently for 10 minutes.

- Add pepper to taste.

- Serve garnished with parsley.

Chicken, risoni and leek soup

Serves 4–6

Risoni looks a little like rice but it's actually a pasta. It makes an ideal addition to all sorts of meat and vegetable soups to make them even more hearty.

2 leeks, thoroughly washed and chopped

400 g chicken fillet (skin and fat removed), diced

2 litres basic chicken stock (page 16), roasted chicken stock (page 18) or miso stock (page 23)

¼ cup risoni pasta

¼ cup dry white wine

freshly ground black pepper

finely chopped fresh herbs (parsley, chives, dill, coriander) to garnish

- In a heavy-based pan, fat-free cook (see page 12) leeks until they begin to soften and brown.

- Add chicken and cook for 5 minutes.

- Add stock and bring to the boil. Then add risoni and simmer for 20 to 30 minutes or until risoni is just cooked.

- Add wine and cook a further 2 to 3 minutes.

- Add pepper to taste.

- Serve garnished with herbs.

Chicken and vegetable soup

Serves 4–6

Keep your eye out for free-range chickens. They have their own unique flavour, without added hormones!

300 g chicken fillet (skin and fat removed), diced

1 onion, peeled and sliced

2 teaspoons finely chopped fresh ginger

1 teaspoon crushed garlic

1 teaspoon finely chopped lemon rind

100 g carrot, chopped

100 g celery, chopped

100 g French beans, cut into 4-cm lengths

100 g red capsicum, seeded and sliced

100 g yellow capsicum, seeded and sliced

½ cup tomato paste

2 teaspoons basil

1 teaspoon oregano

1 litre basic chicken stock (page 16), roasted chicken stock (page 18) or miso stock (page 23)

1 cup dry white wine

freshly ground black pepper

finely chopped fresh herbs (parsley, chives, dill, coriander)

- In a heavy-based pan, fat-free cook (see page 12) chicken, onion, ginger, garlic and lemon until onion is soft and chicken begins to brown. Remove ingredients from pan, cover and keep warm.

- Add vegetables, tomato paste, herbs and stock to the pan. Bring to the boil, cover and simmer for 20 to 30 minutes or until vegetables are soft.

- Return the cooked chicken and onion to the pan along with the wine and slowly bring to the boil.

- Add pepper to taste.

- Stir through the herbs and serve.

Chilled carrot and tomato soup

Serves 4–6

A perfectly delicious summer soup.

1 kg baby carrots

1 kg ripe tomatoes

2 cloves garlic, peeled

2 tablespoons tomato paste

¼ cup fresh basil leaves

pinch salt

freshly ground black pepper to taste

- Thoroughly wash carrots and tomatoes and juice them in a fruit and vegetable juicer.

- Place carrot and tomato juice, garlic, tomato paste and basil in a food processor and blend until smooth.

- Add salt and pepper to taste, and serve.

Note For variation, add some low-fat coconut milk and finely chopped fresh coriander.

Chilled cream of red pepper and tomato soup

Serves 4–6

Simple and sensational.

300 g baby carrots

1 kg ripe tomatoes

1 kg red capsicum, seeded, chargrilled and chopped

2 cloves garlic, peeled

2 tablespoons tomato paste

2 teaspoons sweet chilli sauce

2 teaspoons organic honey

1 cup low-fat yoghurt

pinch salt

freshly ground black pepper

finely chopped fresh basil to garnish

- Thoroughly wash carrots and tomatoes and juice them in a fruit and vegetable juicer.

- Place carrot and tomato juice, capsicum, garlic, tomato paste, sweet chilli sauce, honey and yoghurt in a food processor and blend until smooth.

- Add salt and pepper to taste.

- Serve garnished with basil.

Chilled cucumber, avocado and dill soup

Serves 4–6

A thick soup that's low in fat, high in protein and dietary fibre and loaded with carbohydrate energy.

4–6 Granny Smith apples, peeled and cored

flesh of 2 ripe avocados

1 cup low-fat yoghurt or low-fat coconut milk or half yoghurt and half coconut milk

2 cucumbers, peeled, seeded and grated

1 teaspoon finely grated lemon rind

2 tablespoons finely chopped fresh dill

freshly ground black pepper

extra sprigs of fresh dill to garnish

- Juice apples in a fruit and vegetable juicer.

- Place apple juice, avocado and yoghurt or coconut milk in a food processor and blend until smooth.

- Stir in the cucumber, lemon rind and dill.

- Add pepper to taste.

- Serve garnished with extra dill.

Chilli bean and tomato soup

Serves 6–8

Thick and nourishing enough to be the main meal. If soup becomes too thick, add a little extra stock or red or white wine.

2 onions, peeled and thinly sliced

3 sticks celery, thinly sliced

2 x 810 g cans salt-free tomatoes and juice, puréed

1 litre basic chicken stock (page 16)

1 tablespoon sweet chilli sauce

2 tablespoons tomato paste

1 tablespoon basil

2 x 300 g cans red kidney beans, rinsed and well drained

low-fat yoghurt to garnish

finely chopped fresh coriander or chives to garnish

- In a heavy-based pan, fat-free cook (see page 12) onion until it begins to soften and brown.

- Add celery, tomatoes, stock, chilli sauce, tomato paste and basil. Bring to the boil and simmer uncovered for 20 minutes.

- Purée a cup of the red kidney beans and stir it into the soup. Add remaining beans and cook a further 10 minutes or until beans are heated through and soup has thickened.

- Serve garnished with low-fat yoghurt and coriander or chives.

Chinese carrot and lemon grass soup with crunchy cumin prawns

Serves 4–6

Even if you only ever use Chinese five-spice powder for this recipe, it's well and truly worth keeping a jar of it on your pantry shelf. You can substitute scallops or calamari for the prawns, but grill them as you would the prawns for the best flavour.

24–36 prawns, peeled and deveined, with tails intact

1 tablespoon olive oil

1 tablespoon cumin

1 teaspoon crushed garlic

1 teaspoon finely chopped ginger

2 onions, peeled and diced

800 g carrots, chopped

1 tablespoon finely chopped fresh ginger

1 tablespoon finely chopped lemon grass

1 teaspoon Chinese five-spice powder

1.5 litres basic chicken stock (page 16) or Asian chicken stock (page 17)

½–1 cup freshly squeezed orange juice

finely chopped fresh coriander to garnish

- Combine prawns, oil, cumin, garlic and ginger in a bowl and allow to stand for at least 30 minutes.

- Combine all other ingredients except orange juice and coriander in a large soup pot. Bring to the boil, cover and simmer for 20 to 30 minutes or until carrots are soft. Purée soup.

- Add orange juice and reheat, but do not boil.

- Just before serving, quickly grill prawns under a hot griller or on a hot chargrill pan for just a few minutes.

- Serve garnished with coriander.

Corn and buttermilk soup

Corn is not a vegetable, as most people think. It is, in fact, a cereal. Corn is rich in protein, vitamins B and C and essential fibre. But best of all, it has a wonderful flavour, especially when roasted. Roasting takes a little extra time, but the end result is worth it.

6–8 fresh corn cobs, in their husks	2 cups buttermilk
1 onion, peeled and chopped	freshly ground black pepper
2 cups basic chicken stock (page 16) or light vegetable stock (page 26)	finely chopped fresh chives to garnish
1 yellow capsicum, seeded, chargrilled and chopped	

- Peel back the corn husks (but do not remove them) and strip away the silk. Fold back the husks and tie with string if necessary. Dry-roast (see page 12) corn in a hot oven or over a barbecue or hot coals (for a smoky flavour), until corn is soft and tender. Allow the cobs to cool before peeling away the husks and cutting the corn kernels from the stems.

- In a shallow heavy-based pan, fat-free cook (see page 12) onion until it begins to soften and brown.

- Add stock, corn (reserve a little to use as a garnish) and capsicum and bring to the boil. Purée soup.

- Add buttermilk and reheat, but do not boil.

- Add black pepper to taste.

- Serve garnished with reserved corn kernels and chives.

Creamy asparagus soup

Serves 4–6

In winter and autumn when fresh asparagus is out of season and you have a yearning for a bowl of creamy smooth asparagus soup, be on the look-out for the best canned asparagus available. Canning has little effect on the nutritional value and can actually intensify the asparagus flavour.

1 onion, peeled and chopped

2 tablespoons unbleached plain flour

1½ cups basic fish stock (page 19) or basic chicken stock (page 16)

2 x 340 g cans asparagus and liquid

3 cups low-fat milk or buttermilk

freshly ground black pepper

finely chopped fresh chives or dill to garnish

- In a small heavy-based pan, fat-free cook (see page 12) onion until soft.

- Add flour and cook for 3 to 4 minutes, being careful not to burn it.

- Add stock a little at a time, stirring continuously as it boils and thickens.

- Purée asparagus with asparagus liquid and stir in to onion stock mixture, heating gently. Add milk and reheat, but do not boil.

- Add pepper to taste.

- Serve garnished with chives or dill.

Creamy broccoli and leek soup

Serves 6–8

A smooth soup rich in vitamin C and calcium.

1 leek, thoroughly washed and chopped

1 kg broccoli, chopped

1.5 litres dark vegetable stock (page 25) or basic chicken stock (page 16)

freshly ground black pepper

150 g low-fat ricotta cheese, roughly chopped

½ teaspoon nutmeg to garnish

2 teaspoons parmesan cheese to garnish

- Combine all ingredients except ricotta cheese, nutmeg and parmesan cheese, in a large soup pot. Bring to the boil, cover and simmer for 15 minutes or until broccoli is tender and still a vibrant green. Purée until smooth.

- Place 1 cup of soup mixture and ricotta cheese in a food processor and blend until thick and creamy. Stir this back into the soup and reheat, but do not boil.

- Serve garnished with nutmeg and parmesan cheese.

Creamy chicken and corn soup

Serves 4–6

If fresh corn is available use it in this recipe instead of canned corn. Simply cut the sweet kernels from the cob and add them to the soup at the same time you would have added the canned corn. For a smoky corn flavour you might like to barbecue or grill the corn while still in their husks. Then simply peel away the husks and fibrous matter before removing the kernels and adding them to the soup, just prior to puréeing.

1 onion, peeled and chopped

250 g chicken fillet (skin and fat removed), cut into bite-sized pieces

½ teaspoon turmeric

1 teaspoon finely chopped fresh ginger

½ teaspoon sesame oil

1 yellow capsicum, seeded and chopped

200 g potato, peeled and chopped

1 litre basic chicken stock (page 16) or light vegetable stock (page 26)

1 x 440 g can corn kernels, well drained

finely chopped fresh chives to garnish

- In a shallow heavy-based pan, fat-free cook (see page 12) onion, chicken, turmeric and ginger until onion is soft and chicken is beginning to brown.

- Add sesame oil, capsicum, potato and stock. Bring to the boil, cover and simmer for 20 to 30 minutes.

- Add corn, reserving a couple of spoonfuls to use as a garnish.

- Cook a further 5 to 10 minutes or until corn is heated through. Purée soup.

- Serve garnished with reserved corn and chives.

Creamy chicken soup

Creamy chicken

Serves 4–6

Garlic, garam masala and cumin marry wonderfully in this recipe to produce a warm, aromatic soup.

2 onions, peeled and chopped

2 teaspoons crushed garlic

300 g chicken fillet (skin and fat removed), cut into bite-sized pieces

1 teaspoon garam masala

1 teaspoon cumin

400 g potato, peeled and chopped

1 litre basic chicken stock (page 16) or light vegetable stock (page 26)

1 cup low-fat milk or ½ cup low-fat milk and ½ cup coconut milk

finely chopped fresh chives or thyme to garnish

- In a shallow heavy-based pan, fat-free cook (see page 12) onions, garlic, chicken and spices until onions are soft and chicken is beginning to brown.

- Add potato and stock. Bring to the boil, cover and simmer for 20 to 30 minutes. Purée soup.

- Stir in milk and reheat, but do not boil.

- Serve garnished with chives or thyme.

Creamy curried fish soup

I am a big fan of sea perch. It poaches beautifully and has no bones – just a lovely sweet fish flavour. You can use other varieties of firm white fish in this soup, and each will produce a slightly different flavour. Simply make sure the fish is fresh and remove any bones before making the soup.

1 onion, peeled and diced

1–2 teaspoons curry powder

½ teaspoon cumin

½ teaspoon ground coriander

½ teaspoon garam masala

3 cups basic fish stock (page 19)

200 g potatoes, peeled and chopped

600 g white fish fillets, chopped

1 cup white wine

1 cup low-fat evaporated milk or buttermilk

finely chopped fresh chives or coriander to garnish

- In a heavy-based pan, fat-free cook (see page 12) onion and spices until onion is soft and spices are fragrant.

- Add stock and potato. Bring to the boil, cover and simmer until potato is soft.

- Add fish, cover and simmer until fish is tender. Purée soup in small batches with a little wine.

- Add milk and reheat, but do not boil.

- Serve garnished with chives or coriander.

Creamy mushroom soup

Serves 4–6

You can make this soup with cultivated mushrooms, wild mushrooms or a combination of different varieties. Whichever you use, remember: when you peel mushrooms, you peel away most of the flavour!

1 leek, thoroughly washed and chopped

2 teaspoons crushed garlic

800 g mushrooms, wiped clean with a damp cloth and roughly chopped

2 tablespoons unbleached plain flour

1½ cups beef stock (page 21) or basic chicken stock (page 16)

sprig of fresh thyme

2½ cups low-fat milk or buttermilk

½ cup sherry

freshly ground black pepper

finely chopped fresh parsley or chives to garnish

- In a small heavy-based pan, fat-free cook (see page 12) leek, garlic and mushrooms until they begin to soften and brown.

- Add flour and cook for 3 to 4 minutes, being careful not to burn it.

- Add stock a little at a time, stirring continuously as it boils and thickens. Remove thyme and purée soup.

- Add milk and reheat, but do not boil. Add sherry.

- Add pepper to taste.

- Serve garnished with parsley or chives.

Curried cauliflower soup

Serves 4–6

You may have read that cauliflower is sometimes referred to as the 'aristocrat' of the cabbage family, but trust me – you don't have to be an aristocrat to enjoy this soup. It's as easy to prepare as it is economical, especially in winter when cauliflower is in season.

1 onion, peeled and diced

2 teaspoons crushed garlic

2 teaspoons curry powder

1 teaspoon cumin

½ teaspoon ground coriander

½ teaspoon cinnamon

1 teaspoon sesame oil

1 medium cauliflower, roughly chopped

2 cups basic chicken stock (page 16)

2 cups low-fat evaporated milk or buttermilk

freshly ground black pepper

finely chopped fresh chives or coriander to garnish

- In a heavy-based pan, sauté onion, garlic and spices in sesame oil until onion is soft and spices are fragrant.

- Add cauliflower and stock. Bring to the boil, cover and simmer for 15 to 20 minutes or until cauliflower is soft. Purée soup.

- Add milk and reheat, but do not boil.

- Add pepper to taste.

- Serve garnished with chives or coriander.

Curried parsnip soup

Serves 4–6

Roasted parsnips and a little coconut milk gives this soup a whole new image!

2 onions, peeled and diced

2 teaspoons crushed garlic

2 teaspoons vindaloo curry paste

1 teaspoon cumin

¼ teaspoon ground fenugreek

700 g parsnip, topped and tailed and chopped

100 g potato, peeled and chopped

2 cups beef stock (page 21) or miso stock (page 23)

2 cups low-fat evaporated milk or buttermilk

freshly ground black pepper

finely chopped fresh chives or coriander to garnish

- In a heavy-based pan, fat-free cook (see page 12) onions, garlic, curry paste and spices until onion is soft and spices are fragrant.

- Add parsnip, potato and stock. Bring to the boil, cover and simmer for 15 to 20 minutes or until parsnip and potato are soft. Purée soup.

- Add milk and reheat, but do not boil.

- Add pepper to taste.

- Serve garnished with chives or coriander.

Curried scallop and sweet potato soup

Serves 6–8

A deliciously wonderful soup created for an exceptionally wonderful man who just loves scallops – my Dad.

2 onions, peeled and diced

1 tablespoon curry powder

½ teaspoon cumin

½ teaspoon cinnamon

1 tablespoon tomato paste

800 g sweet potato, peeled and chopped

200 g potato, peeled and chopped

1 litre basic chicken stock (page 16)

500 g scallops (fresh or frozen)

1 cup white wine

½–1 cup low-fat milk

freshly ground black pepper

finely chopped fresh chives to garnish

- Combine all ingredients except scallops, wine, milk, pepper and chives in a large soup pot. Bring to the boil, cover and simmer for 30 to 40 minutes or until potato is soft.

- Blanch (see page 11) scallops in wine. Remove all but 8 scallops from the pan and cover. Add the 8 scallops with cooking liquid to the soup and purée until smooth.

- Add pepper to taste.

- Serve garnished with whole cooked scallops and chives.

Note If you can't find fresh scallops, frozen scallops are just as good. They thaw out easily and quickly in a bowl of cold water.

Curried sweet potato and carrot soup

Serves 4–6

A rich, warm and aromatic soup with Indian undertones.

1 onion, peeled and diced

1 tablespoon red curry paste

2 teaspoons crushed garlic

1 teaspoon cumin

½ teaspoon turmeric

½ teaspoon cinnamon

400 g sweet potato, peeled and chopped

300 g carrots, chopped

200 g potato, peeled and chopped

1 litre dark vegetable stock (page 25), light vegetable stock (page 26) or basic chicken stock (page 16)

1 cup low-fat yoghurt to garnish

grated orange rind to garnish

finely chopped fresh coriander to garnish

- Combine all ingredients except yoghurt, orange rind and coriander in a large soup pot. Bring to the boil, cover and simmer for 30 to 40 minutes or until vegetables are soft.

- Purée soup until thick and smooth.

- Serve garnished with yoghurt, orange rind and coriander.

Dahl corn soup

Serves 6–8

A thick soup that is low in fat, high in protein and dietary fibre, and loaded with carbohydrate energy. Cook it slowly to allow the best flavours to evolve.

1 x 500 g packet yellow split peas

1 onion, peeled and diced

1 tablespoon red curry paste

1 teaspoon crushed garlic

1 teaspoon cumin

½ teaspoon turmeric

½ teaspoon cinnamon

corn from 2 corn cobs or 1 x 425 g can corn kernels, well drained

2 x 425 g cans salt-free tomatoes and juice

1 carrot, grated

2.5 litres dark vegetable stock (page 25), light vegetable stock (page 26) or basic chicken stock (page 16)

freshly ground black pepper

finely chopped fresh herbs (parsley, chives, coriander) to garnish

- Rinse split peas in cold water. Discard any discoloured peas or foreign material. Leave to soak overnight or for a few hours before cooking. While soaking is not absolutely necessary, it will reduce the cooking time by approximately half an hour.

- Place all ingredients except pepper and fresh herbs in a large soup pot. Bring to the boil, then turn heat down and very gently simmer for 1 to 1½ hours or until peas are quite soft and the soup thick. Stir often to prevent peas sticking to the base of pot.

- Add pepper to taste.

- Serve garnished with herbs.

Eggplant soup

Serves 4–6

The eggplant takes centre-stage here, and deservedly. They are rich in vitamin C and provide small amounts of iron. Choose firm, smooth and shiny black- or purple-skinned eggplants for this recipe. Young eggplants tend not to be bitter and rarely need degorging.

3 eggplants

2 onions, peeled and diced

1 carrot, finely chopped

1 tablespoon crushed garlic

2 tablespoons olive oil

2 cups basic chicken stock (page 16), dark vegetable stock (page 25) or miso stock (page 23)

2 teaspoons basil

1 tablespoon low-salt soy sauce

2 tablespoons sherry

1–2 cups low-fat evaporated milk or buttermilk

freshly ground black pepper

chopped chives or parsley to garnish

- Degorge eggplants (see page 12) then chargrill (page 11) and roughly chop.

- Sauté onions, carrot and garlic in olive oil until onion and carrot begin to soften and brown.

- Add stock, basil, soy sauce and sherry and bring to the boil. Then add eggplant and purée soup until thick and creamy.

- Add enough milk for desired consistency and reheat, but do not boil.

- Add pepper to taste.

- Serve garnished with chives or parsley.

Fennel, fish and tomato soup

Serves 4–6

The aniseed flavour of fennel turns fish into a fast, tasty feast.

400 g – 600 g firm white fish fillets, cut into bite-sized pieces

½ cup basic fish stock (page 19) or white wine

2 bay leaves

1 tablespoon olive oil

1 onion, peeled and diced

1 stick celery, finely chopped

1 carrot, finely diced

2 teaspoons crushed garlic

400 g fennel (white part only), chopped

600 g ripe tomatoes

2 tablespoons tomato paste

1 tablespoon apple juice concentrate

1.5 litres basic fish stock (page 19) or basic chicken stock (page 16)

finely chopped fresh fennel (green feathery tops only) to garnish

- Place fish, stock or wine and bay leaves in a small pan. Cover and cook fish until it is just tender. Remove fish, strain the cooking liquid and reserve.

- In a heavy-based pan, add olive oil, onion, celery, carrot, garlic and fennel. Cover and cook until all vegetables are quite soft.

- Add tomatoes, tomato paste, apple juice concentrate, stock and reserved cooking liquid. Bring to the boil then simmer for 20 to 30 minutes or until tomatoes have broken down and soup begins to thicken.

- Purée half the soup and return it to the pot.

- Place cooked fish in individual bowls and ladle over the soup.

- Serve garnished with fennel.

Fennel, leek and potato soup

Serves 6–8

If you haven't eaten fennel before, this is a good introduction. It has a unique aniseed flavour that marries well with potatoes and leeks.

2 small leeks (white part only), thoroughly washed and chopped

400 g fennel (white part only), chopped

600 g potato, peeled and chopped

1.5 litres dark vegetable stock (page 25), light vegetable stock (page 26) or beef stock (page 21)

¼ cup pernod

½ cup low-fat milk

pinch salt

freshly ground black pepper

2 tablespoons finely chopped fresh fennel (green feathery tops only) to garnish

- Combine all ingredients except pernod, milk, salt, pepper and fennel (for garnish) in a large soup pot. Bring to the boil, cover and simmer for 30 to 40 minutes or until vegetables are soft. Purée soup.

- Heat pernod in a small saucepan until it boils. Stir in to the soup along with the milk.

- Add salt and pepper to taste.

- Serve garnished with fennel.

Fishy soup

Serves 6–8

A rich flavoured fish soup relies on a good fish stock and minimal cooking of any fresh fish that you add just prior to serving.

1 onion, peeled and diced

1 x 425 g can salt-free tomatoes and juice, puréed

½ cup tomato paste

1 teaspoon dried basil

1 teaspoon dried mint

1 litre basic fish stock (page 19) or fragrant fish stock (page 20)

½–1 cup dry white wine

100 g celery, thinly sliced

100 g carrot, cut into thin rounds

100 g zucchini, cut into thin rounds

800 g mixed fish (prawns, scallops and any firm white fish fillets)

2 spring onions, thinly diagonally sliced

freshly ground black pepper

finely chopped fresh herbs (mint, parsley, basil) to garnish

- Combine the first 6 ingredients in a large soup pot. Bring to the boil, cover and simmer for 10 minutes.

- Add wine and vegetables and continue to cook a further 10 minutes or until vegetables are just soft.

- Remove shells from prawns and devein. Wash scallops in cold water, remove brown vein and leave orange roe on. Remove any bone and skin from fish fillets and cut into bite-sized pieces.

- Add mixed fish and cook for a few minutes or until fish is just cooked. Be careful not to overcook the fish: it will continue cooking once served.

- Add pepper to taste.

- Serve garnished with herbs.

Gazpacho

This recipe appeared in my first book, Taste of Life. *I've made just a couple of small changes. You know what they say, 'When you're on a good thing, stick with it', and that's exactly how I feel about this combination of ingredients. The tomatoes must be ripe to get the best flavour, and don't attempt to make this with out-of-season tomatoes as you will be disappointed.*

500 g ripe tomatoes, peeled, seeded and chopped

1 small red onion, peeled and finely diced

1 green capsicum, seeded and finely diced

1 small Lebanese cucumber, peeled and seeded

½ cup dry white wine

1 cup salt-free tomato juice

1 teaspoon crushed garlic

1–2 teaspoons freshly squeezed lemon juice

pinch cayenne pepper

freshly ground black pepper

pinch salt

1 tablespoon finely chopped fresh dill

- Process the first 4 ingredients in a food processor. Do not purée the vegetables completely as the soup should be a little crunchy.

- Stir in the wine and tomato juice.

- Add garlic, lemon juice, cayenne pepper, and black pepper and salt to taste.

- Stir through the dill and refrigerate for at least 2 hours to allow the flavours to develop before serving.

Green pea and apple curry soup

Serves 6–8

This is a little like pea and ham soup – without the ham bone – and full of that good fibre we all need every day. Serve it with pumpkin, polenta and lemon grass damper (page 125).

500 g packet green split peas

200 g leek, thoroughly washed and chopped

1 teaspoon finely chopped fresh ginger

3 teaspoons green curry paste

1 potato, peeled and chopped

2 Granny Smith apples, peeled, cored and chopped

2 litres dark vegetable stock (page 25), light vegetable stock (page 26) or basic chicken stock (page 16)

1 cup low-fat yoghurt to garnish

finely chopped fresh coriander and mint to garnish

1 Fuji or Jonathan apple, cored and thinly sliced to garnish

- Rinse split peas in cold water. Discard any discoloured peas or foreign material. Leave to soak overnight or for a few hours before cooking. While soaking is not absolutely necessary, it will reduce the cooking time by approximately half an hour.

- Combine the first 7 ingredients in a large soup pot. Bring to the boil, cover and simmer until peas are soft and soup is quite thick.

- Remove from heat and purée until smooth.

- Serve garnished with a spoonful of yoghurt, topped with herbs and apple slices.

Green pea, basil and mint soup

Serves 4–6

An ideal soup for a light lunch with friends on a lazy Saturday afternoon. Serve it with fresh crusty wholemeal bread or sun-dried tomato, olive and onion damper (page 127) and an antipasto platter.

500 g packet green split peas

1 onion, peeled and chopped

2 sticks celery, chopped

2 teaspoons crushed garlic

2 teaspoons basil

1 litre light vegetable stock
(page 26) or basic chicken stock
(page 16)

2 cups water

½ cup coconut milk

1 tablespoon finely chopped fresh mint

- Rinse split peas in cold water. Discard any discoloured peas or foreign material. Leave to soak overnight or for a few hours before cooking. While soaking is not absolutely necessary, it will reduce the cooking time by approximately half an hour.

- Combine the first 7 ingredients in a large soup pot. Bring to the boil, cover and simmer for approximately 40 minutes or until peas are soft and soup is quite thick.

- Remove from heat and purée until smooth.

- Stir through the coconut milk and mint, and serve.

Hungarian chicken and two potato soup

Serves 6–8

Warm in colour and warm on taste.

1 cup red lentils

1 onion, peeled and thinly sliced

2 teaspoons finely chopped fresh ginger

400 g chicken fillet (skin and fat removed), finely diced

2 teaspoons paprika

2 teaspoons cumin

½ teaspoon cinnamon

300 g potato, peeled and cut into thin julienne strips

300 g sweet potato, peeled and cut into thin julienne strips

1 litre dark vegetable stock (page 25), Vecon stock (page 23) or basic chicken stock (page 16)

3 cups water

1 cup red wine

1 x 140 g tub tomato paste

¼–½ cup finely chopped fresh parsley

- Rinse lentils in cold water. Discard any discoloured lentils or foreign material.

- In a heavy-based pan, fat-free cook (see page 12) onion, ginger and chicken until onion is soft and chicken begins to brown.

- Add lentils, spices, vegetables, stock, water, wine and tomato paste, cover and bring to the boil. Stir well. Simmer, stirring occasionally, for 30 to 40 minutes or until vegetables are soft and soup has thickened.

- Stir through the parsley and serve.

Lamb shank and barley soup

Serves 4–6

Barley is an exceptionally nutritious grain. It's rich in niacin, thiamine, folate, iron, magnesium and zinc. It's also high in fibre; but best of all it tastes terrific. It turns an ordinary lamb shank soup into a wholesome meal.

1 tablespoon miso paste

½ cup boiling water

1 onion, peeled and finely chopped

½ cup pearl barley

100 g zucchini, grated

100 g carrot, grated

100 g swede, peeled and grated

100 g turnip, peeled and grated

½ teaspoon thyme

1 litre lamb shank stock (page 22)

100 g cooked lamb shank meat

finely ground black pepper

¼–½ cup finely chopped fresh parsley

- Dissolve miso paste in boiling water.

- Combine miso, onion, pearl barley, vegetables, thyme and stock in a large soup pot. Bring to the boil, cover and simmer for an hour or until barley and vegetables are soft.

- Add lamb shank meat and cook a further 10 minutes.

- Add pepper to taste.

- Stir through the herbs and serve.

Lamb shank soup

Serves 6–8

An old favourite soup recipe that turns inexpensive lamb shanks and fresh winter vegetables into a warming winter meal.

2 litres lamb shank stock (page 22)

1 tablespoon crushed garlic

500 g leek, thoroughly washed and chopped

500 g carrot, chopped

500 g zucchini, chopped

200 g potato, peeled and chopped

200 g parsnip, chopped

200 g swede, peeled and chopped

200 g turnip, peeled and chopped

2 x 425 g cans salt-free tomatoes and juice

pinch ground rosemary or a sprig of fresh rosemary

200 g cooked lamb shank meat

1 x 300 g can chick peas (well drained) or 1 cup cooked brown lentils or 1 cup cooked red kidney beans (well drained)

finely ground black pepper

¼–½ cup finely chopped fresh herbs (parsley, chives, thyme, marjoram)

- Combine all ingredients except lamb shank meat, chick peas, pepper and herbs. Bring to the boil and simmer, uncovered, for 1 to 1½ hours or until vegetables are soft and soup begins to reduce and thicken.

- Remove rosemary sprig and discard.

- Add lamb shank meat and chick peas and cook a further 10 minutes.

- Add pepper to taste.

- Stir through the herbs and serve.

Lemon bean soup

Serves 4

Just a few ingredients come to life fast in a deliciously lemony way.

2 onions, peeled and diced

1 tablespoon finely chopped lemon grass

1 teaspoon turmeric

½ teaspoon curry powder

1 tablespoon olive oil

2 x 300 g cans butter beans, rinsed and well drained

1 litre basic chicken stock (page 16)

finely chopped fresh parsley and chives to garnish

- In a heavy-based pan, sauté onions, lemon grass, turmeric, curry powder and olive oil until onions and lemon grass are soft and spices quite fragrant.

- Purée beans.

- Stir beans and stock into onion mixture. Bring to the boil, cover and simmer, stirring occasionally, for 15 to 20 minutes.

- Serve garnished with parsley and chives.

Lunch-in-a-bowl soup

Serves 6–8

Who could have imagined there was so much flavour in a packet of bean soup mix?

250 g packet of bean soup mix

2 onions, peeled and diced

2 sticks celery, chopped

2 potatoes, peeled and chopped

2 carrots, chopped

500 g pumpkin, peeled and chopped

1 x 425 g can salt-free tomatoes and juice

2 teaspoons mixed herbs

3 litres light vegetable stock (page 26), basic chicken stock (page 16) or beef stock (page 21)

1 zucchini, cut into rounds

100 g French beans, cut into 4-cm lengths

100 g broccoli florets

freshly ground black pepper

finely chopped fresh herbs (parsley, chives, oregano, thyme, marjoram) to garnish

- Rinse soup mix in cold water. Discard any discoloured grains or foreign material. Leave to soak overnight or for a few hours before cooking. While soaking is not absolutely necessary, it will reduce the cooking time by approximately half an hour.

- Combine the first 9 ingredients in a large soup pot. Bring to the boil, cover and gently simmer for 1 to 1½ hours or until grains are quite soft.

- Add zucchini, beans and broccoli and cook a further 20 to 30 minutes.

- Add pepper to taste.

- Serve garnished with herbs.

Melon soup

Serves 4–6

Light and refreshing!

500 g cantaloup flesh	2 teaspoons honey
500 g honeydew melon flesh	2 spring onions, finely chopped
2 Granny Smith apples, peeled and cored	1 tablespoon finely chopped fresh mint
5-cm piece fresh ginger, peeled	2 teaspoons finely chopped fresh coriander

- Juice cantaloup, honeydew melon, apples and ginger in a fruit and vegetable juicer.

- Warm the honey.

- Stir through the honey, spring onions and herbs, and serve.

Minestrone

Serves 6–8

Actually more like a stew than a soup.

1–2 teaspoons crushed garlic

1 onion, peeled and chopped

2 large carrots, cut into rounds

2 sticks celery, thinly sliced

1 large potato, peeled and cubed

20 French beans, topped and tailed and cut into four pieces each

2 small zucchini, cut into rounds

1 red capsicum, seeded and roughly chopped

1 x 425 g can salt-free tomatoes and juice

2 litres dark vegetable stock (page 25), light vegetable stock (page 26) or Vecon stock (page 23)

¼ cup salt-free tomato paste

1 teaspoon basil

½ teaspoon oregano

½ teaspoon marjoram

¼ teaspoon thyme

pinch salt

freshly ground black pepper

1 cup cold cooked pasta (ribbons, macaroni, rigatoni, shells, spirals)

1 x 425 g can red kidney beans, rinsed and well drained

1 cup chopped fresh parsley

- Combine all ingredients except pasta, kidney beans and parsley in a large soup pot. Slowly bring to the boil, cover and simmer for approximately 2½ hours.

- Add pasta and beans and cook uncovered a further 15 minutes, stirring every few minutes to prevent beans and pasta sticking to the base of pot.

- Stir through the parsley and serve.

Miso, nori and noodle soup

Serves 4–6

Shiitake mushrooms, also known as Chinese mushrooms, do not have the same nutritional value as the ordinary field mushroom, but they do have a unique flavour that makes them an ideal choice for this Japanese-style soup. Nori brings the smell of the ocean and the flavour of the sea just a little closer to your front door. It's rich in minerals, a good source of calcium and considered an important staple of an Asian diet.

200 g fresh hokkein noodles

2 tablespoons miso paste

1 cup boiling water

7 cups cold water

2 tablespoons salt-free tomato paste

1 tablespoon finely chopped fresh ginger

1 tablespoon finely chopped lemon grass

2 tablespoons low-salt soy sauce

1 tablespoon fish sauce

2 tablespoons apple juice concentrate

1 red capsicum, seeded and cut into thin strips

200 g snow peas, topped and tailed

20 shiitake mushrooms, sliced

100 g spinach, chopped

freshly ground black pepper

2–4 sheets nori seaweed (black or green), cut into thin strips

4 spring onions, thinly diagonally sliced

1 x 375 g packet silken tofu, cubed

finely chopped fresh flat-leaf parsley to garnish

- Pour boiling water over noodles in a large bowl and allow them to soak for 2 to 3 minutes or until soft. Drain well.

- Dissolve miso paste in boiling water.

- Place cold water, tomato paste, ginger, lemon grass, soy sauce, fish sauce and apple juice concentrate in a large soup pot and bring to the boil.

- Add capsicum and snow peas and simmer until they are just tender.

- Add mushrooms and cook a further 1 minute. Then add spinach and pepper to taste.

- Place nori, spring onions and tofu in individual soup bowls.

- Ladle over the soup.

- Serve immediately garnished with parsley.

Miso, vegetable and tofu soup

Serves 4

Keep some miso paste in the refrigerator and a packet of silken tofu in the pantry so you can make a nutritious, tasty soup in absolutely no time at all. This is my on-the-run lunchtime soup, my pick-me-up dinner soup after a long day and my all-round energy tonic! You won't find any ingredients here that get in the way of your concentration and stamina; in fact it could almost be called the Brilliant Brain Soup!

2 tablespoons miso paste

1 cup boiling water

5 cups cold water

1 tablespoon salt-free tomato paste

2 zucchini, sliced into rounds

2 carrots, sliced into rounds

3 sticks celery, chopped

1 bunch asparagus spears, trimmed, cut into 4-cm lengths

1 teaspoon oregano

1 teaspoon basil

10 shiitake mushrooms, sliced

1 x 375 g packet silken tofu, cubed

freshly ground black pepper

finely chopped fresh flat-leaf parsley to garnish

- Dissolve miso paste in boiling water.

- Place cold water, tomato paste, zucchini, carrots, celery, asparagus, oregano and basil in a large soup pot. Bring to the boil, cover and simmer until vegetables are just tender.

- Add mushrooms and cook a further 2 minutes. Then add tofu to warm through.

- Add pepper to taste.

- Serve immediately garnished with parsley.

Mushroom and beef soup

Serves 4–6

This recipe is perfect for both field and cultivated mushrooms. Why not try a mixture of fresh and dried?

500 g mushrooms, wiped clean with a damp cloth and chopped

2 onions, peeled, halved and thinly sliced

2 teaspoons crushed garlic

1 carrot, cut into thin julienne strips

1 potato, peeled and diced

1 tablespoon tamari

2 tablespoons dry sherry

1 litre beef stock (page 21), miso stock or Vecon stock (both page 23)

freshly ground black pepper

4 diagonally sliced spring onions to garnish

- In a shallow heavy-based pan, fat-free cook (see page 12) mushrooms, onions and garlic until they begin to soften and brown.

- Add carrot, potato, tamari, sherry and stock. Bring to the boil, cover and simmer for 15 to 20 minutes.

- Add pepper to taste.

- Serve garnished with spring onions.

Oodles of noodles and vegetable soup

Serves 6–8

Filling without being fattening.

1 onion, peeled and thinly sliced

200 g leek, thoroughly washed and chopped

2 teaspoons crushed garlic

1 teaspoon finely chopped fresh ginger

2 sticks celery, finely sliced

2 carrots, grated

200 g swede, peeled and grated

2 zucchini, cut into thin rounds

200 g pumpkin, peeled and cubed

2 litres light vegetable stock (page 26), Vecon stock or miso stock (both page 23) or basic chicken stock (page 16)

50 g angel hair pasta

freshly ground black pepper

3 finely sliced spring onions to garnish

- In a shallow heavy-based pan, fat-free cook (see page 12) onion, leek, garlic and ginger until they begin to soften and brown.

- Add all other vegetables and stock. Bring to the boil, cover and simmer for 15 to 20 minutes.

- Add pasta and stir through. Return to the boil and simmer until pasta is soft.

- Add pepper to taste.

- Serve garnished with spring onions.

Orange, pumpkin and ginger soup

Serves 4–6

Ginger is incredibly good for your digestion. It also adds just the right flavour to this very simple pumpkin soup recipe.

1 onion, peeled and diced

2 teaspoons cumin

1 tablespoon finely chopped fresh ginger

1 tablespoon finely grated orange zest

1 kg pumpkin, peeled and chopped

1 litre light vegetable stock (page 26) or basic chicken stock (page 16)

1 cup freshly squeezed orange juice

¼ cup white wine

low-fat yoghurt to garnish

¼ cup finely chopped fresh chives

• Combine the first 6 ingredients in a large soup pot. Bring to the boil, cover and simmer until pumpkin is tender. Purée soup.

• Add orange juice and wine and simmer for 3 minutes.

• Serve garnished with swirls of yoghurt topped with chives.

Potato and leek soup

Thick, warm and wonderful.

1 tablespoon Vecon paste

½ cup boiling water

3½ cups cold water

2 teaspoons crushed garlic

200 g leek, thoroughly washed and chopped

2 sticks celery, chopped

4 potatoes, peeled and chopped

finely ground black pepper to taste

pinch salt

1 x 150 ml can low-fat evaporated milk

2 diagonally sliced spring onions, to garnish

- Dissolve Vecon paste in boiling water and add cold water.

- Place all ingredients except evaporated milk in a large soup pot and cook until potato and leek are soft. Purée soup.

- Add milk and reheat, but do not boil.

- Serve garnished with spring onions.

Opposite: Oodles of noodles and vegetable soup (see page 84).

Potato and watercress soup

Serves 4–6

Watercress has a wonderful natural peppery flavour that lifts this soup.

1 teaspoon crushed garlic

200 g leek, thoroughly washed and chopped

2 sticks celery, chopped

400 g potatoes, peeled and chopped

1.5 litres basic chicken stock (page 16) or miso stock (page 23)

400 g watercress

1 extra leek, thoroughly washed and sliced diagonally, to garnish

low-fat yoghurt to garnish

- In a shallow heavy-based pan, fat-free cook (see page 12) garlic, leek and celery until they begin to soften and brown.

- Add potatoes and stock. Bring to the boil, cover and simmer for 15 to 20 minutes or until potato is soft.

- Add watercress and cook a further 5 minutes. Purée soup until thick and creamy.

- In another small, shallow heavy-based pan, fat-free cook the extra chopped leek until it softens and browns a little.

- Serve garnished with yoghurt and extra leek.

Opposite: Red lentil and capsicum soup (see page 93).

Pumpkin, coconut and chick pea soup

Serves 4–6

A perfect combination of ingredients – with just a little crunch.

2 teaspoons finely chopped fresh ginger

1 onion, peeled and diced

500 g pumpkin, peeled and chopped

400 g potato, peeled and chopped

1 litre light vegetable stock (page 26) or basic chicken stock (page 16)

1 x 300 g can chick peas, well drained

140 ml low-fat coconut milk

2 tablespoons finely chopped fresh basil to garnish

- In a heavy-based pan, fat-free cook (see page 12) onion and ginger until onion begins to soften and brown.

- Add pumpkin, potato and stock and cook until vegetables are soft. Purée soup.

- Add chick peas and continue to purée.

- Stir through the coconut milk.

- Serve immediately garnished with basil.

Pumpkin pepper soup

Serves 4–6

A recipe for those who like their pumpkin soups a little hot!

2 onions, peeled and diced

1 red capsicum, seeded and diced

2 teaspoons finely chopped fresh ginger

1 teaspoon crushed garlic

1–2 teaspoons vindaloo curry paste

800 g pumpkin, peeled and chopped

200 g potato, peeled and chopped

1.5 litres light vegetable stock (page 26) or basic chicken stock (page 16)

2 red capsicums, seeded, chargrilled, chopped and puréed, to garnish

- In a heavy-based pan fat-free cook (see page 12) onions, capsicum, ginger, garlic and curry paste until onion and capsicum begin to soften and brown.

- Add pumpkin, potato and stock and cook until vegetables are soft. Purée soup.

- Serve garnished with swirls of puréed red capsicum.

Pumpkin and spinach laksa

Serves 4–6

This spicy laksa recipe makes an ideal vegetarian meal.

200 g rice noodles

800 g pumpkin, peeled and cubed

1 litre light vegetable stock (page 26), boiling

140 ml coconut milk

200 g spinach, roughly chopped

100 g bean shoots

finely chopped fresh basil to garnish

Laksa paste

1 teaspoon vegetable or peanut oil

4 spring onions, finely diced

2 cloves garlic, peeled and crushed

2 teaspoons finely chopped fresh ginger

2–3 small red chillies, seeded and finely chopped

1 tablespoon finely chopped fresh lemon grass (approx. 1 stem, white part only)

6 macadamia nuts, finely diced

½ teaspoon turmeric

2 teaspoons cumin

1 teaspoon ground coriander

1 tablespoon fish sauce

2 tablespoons apple juice concentrate

- Pour boiling water over noodles in a large bowl and allow them to soak for 2 to 3 minutes or until soft. Drain well.

- Blanch (see page 11) pumpkin.

- In a heavy-based pan cook the first 10 ingredients of the laksa paste until onion softens and spices are fragrant. Add remaining ingredients and cook a further minute, stirring continuously.

- Add boiling stock. Simmer for approximately 5 minutes.

- Stir in the coconut milk and heat through, but do not boil.

- Add spinach and cook until spinach has just softened.

- Place equal amounts of cooked rice noodles at the bottom of each soup bowl. Add pumpkin and top with bean shoots.

- Ladle spoonfuls of soup over the noodles and vegetables.

- Serve garnished with basil.

Pumpkin and tomato soup

One of the first soups I ever made as a new bride was pumpkin and tomato. I'm not sure whether it was to impress my new husband or my father-in-law! It still tastes just as good and takes me back to my bright red farm kitchen.

1 onion, peeled and diced

2 teaspoons finely chopped fresh ginger

2 teaspoons crushed garlic

1 kg pumpkin, peeled and chopped

1.5 litres basic chicken stock (page 16)

¼–½ cup tomato paste

2 teaspoons basil

freshly ground black pepper

- Place all ingredients except pepper in a large soup pot. Bring to the boil, cover and simmer until pumpkin is just soft. Purée soup.

- Add lots of pepper to taste and serve.

Red lentil and capsicum soup

Thick, hearty, mildly spicy – and heavenly.

200 g red lentils

2 red capsicums, seeded and chopped

2 onions, peeled and chopped

200 g potato, peeled and chopped

1 teaspoon basil

2 teaspoons cumin

1 x 425 g can salt-free tomatoes and juice, puréed

1 litre light vegetable stock (page 26) or basic chicken stock (page 16)

finely chopped fresh parsley, coriander or basil to garnish

- Rinse lentils in cold water. Discard any discoloured lentils or foreign material.

- Combine all ingredients except herbs (for garnish) in a large soup pot. Bring to the boil, cover and simmer until vegetables and lentils are soft. Purée soup.

- Serve garnished with herbs.

Red roma tomato soup

Serves 4–6

Red roma tomato soup will only taste as good as the tomatoes you use to make it.

1 kg ripe roma tomatoes, roughly chopped

2 onions, peeled and diced

3 teaspoons red curry paste

2 teaspoons finely chopped fresh ginger

1 carrot, chopped

3 tablespoons tomato paste

8 fresh basil leaves

1 litre basic chicken stock (page 16) or light vegetable stock (page 26)

pinch salt

finely chopped fresh basil

- Combine all ingredients except salt and basil in a large soup pot. Bring to the boil, cover and simmer for 50 minutes.

- Remove from heat and purée until smooth.

- Add salt to taste.

- Stir through the herbs and serve.

Roasted garlic and curry carrot soup

Serves 4–6

Roasted garlic will bring a rich, warm and wonderful garlic flavour to your favourite soups. Two or three cloves will bring new meaning to an old favourite soup recipe, but why not really get your tastebuds going with just a few more . . .

2 onions, peeled and diced

1 teaspoon vindaloo curry paste

1 teaspoon finely chopped fresh ginger

1 teaspoon cumin

1 teaspoon garam masala

800 g carrots, chopped

200 g potatoes, peeled and chopped

10 cloves garlic, roasted

1 tablespoon tomato paste

1.5 litres basic chicken stock (page 16), Vecon stock or miso stock (both page 23) or roasted chicken stock (page 18)

fresh coriander leaves to garnish

- In a shallow heavy-based pan, fat-free cook (see page 12) onions, curry paste, ginger and spices until onion is soft.

- Add carrots, potatoes, garlic, tomato paste and stock. Bring to the boil, cover and simmer for 30 minutes or until vegetables are soft. Purée soup until smooth and creamy.

- Remove any garlic casing fibres.

- Serve garnished with coriander.

Roasted garlic and potato soup

Serves 4–6

I first tasted this soup in a wonderful little local café. It was so delicious I simply had to go home that night and find a way to make my very own roasted garlic and potato soup. Serve it with your favourite crusty, grainy breads or a thick slice of mega-grain damper (page 122), and make a meal of it.

1 onion, peeled and diced

750 g potatoes, peeled and chopped

6 cloves garlic, roasted

1 litre beef stock (page 21) or miso stock (page 23)

low-fat yoghurt to garnish (optional)

finely chopped fresh chives to garnish

- Combine all ingredients except yoghurt and chives in a large soup pot. Bring to the boil, cover and simmer for 20 to 30 minutes or until potato is soft. Purée soup.

- Serve garnished with yoghurt and chives.

Scallop and potato soup

Scallops take on a perfectly wonderful flavour with the addition of just a little pernod.

1 large leek, thoroughly washed and chopped

1 kg potatoes, peeled and chopped

1 litre basic fish stock (page 19)

½ cup extra fish stock

2–3 sprigs fresh parsley

400 g scallops

1 cup low-fat milk

¼ cup pernod

freshly ground black pepper

finely chopped fresh parsley to garnish

- Combine leek, potatoes and fish stock in a large soup pot. Bring to the boil, cover and simmer for 20 to 30 minutes or until leek and potato are soft.

- Place extra stock and parsley in a small pan. Bring to a gentle simmer and poach scallops. Remove 8 scallops with orange roe still intact to use as a garnish. Cover them so they do not dry out. Discard extra stock and parsley.

- Purée soup in several batches.

- Stir in the milk and reheat, but do not boil.

- Place pernod in a small saucepan, bring to the boil and then add to soup.

- Add pepper to taste.

- Serve garnished with reserved scallops and parsley.

Seafood and bean curd laksa

Serves 4–6

This laksa recipe combines a range of sensational flavours, some fresh from the sea.

200 g fresh hokkien or udon noodles

200 g bean curd, cut into 1 cm x 3 cm squares

100 g snow peas, cut into thin julienne strips

1 litre light vegetable stock (page 26) or basic fish stock (page 19), boiling

2 fresh kaffir lime leaves or a squeeze of fresh lime juice

750 g mixed seafood (prawns, calamari, octopus, white fish fillet) uncooked, cleaned and chopped

140 ml coconut milk

100 g bean shoots

2 finely sliced spring onions to garnish

fresh coriander and mint to garnish

Laksa paste

1 teaspoon vegetable or sesame oil

1 onion, peeled and finely diced

3 cloves garlic, peeled and crushed

3 teaspoons finely chopped fresh ginger

1 tablespoon finely chopped fresh lemon grass (approx. 1 stem, white part only)

2 teaspoons finely chopped fresh coriander root

½ teaspoon saffron or turmeric

1 teaspoon cumin

2 teaspoons sweet chilli sauce

1½ tablespoons fish sauce

2 tablespoons apple juice concentrate

- Pour boiling water over the noodles in a large bowl and allow them to soak for 2 to 3 minutes or until soft. Drain well.

- Grill bean curd until lightly browned.

- Blanch (see page 11) snow peas.

- In a heavy-based pan, cook the first 8 ingredients of the laksa paste until onion softens and spices are fragrant. Add remaining ingredients and cook a further minute, stirring continuously.

- Add boiling stock and lime leaves or lime juice. Simmer for approximately 5 minutes.

- Add seafood and cook for approximately 2 to 3 minutes or until tender.

- Stir in the coconut milk and heat through, but do not boil.

- Place equal amounts of cooked noodles at the bottom of each soup bowl. Add some snow peas and top with bean shoots.

- Ladle spoonfuls of soup over the noodles and vegetables.

- Serve garnished with spring onions, coriander and mint.

Spicy black bean soup

Serves 4–6

A rich spicy soup that'll warm your whole body. It can be served thick and chunky or puréed and garnished with some low-fat yoghurt or thinned ricotta cheese (see page 1).

2 onions, peeled and finely diced

300 g carrot, finely diced

6 cloves garlic, crushed

1 tablespoon olive oil

2 teaspoons cumin

2 tablespoons black bean paste

2 tablespoons tomato paste

½ cup red wine

1 litre beef stock (page 21)

2 cups cooked black-eyed beans

finely chopped fresh parsley to garnish

- In a shallow heavy-based pan, sauté onions, carrot, garlic, oil and cumin for 10 minutes or until onion and carrot are soft.

- Stir in the black bean paste, tomato paste, red wine and stock and cook for 15 minutes.

- Add black-eyed beans and cook a further 15 minutes.

- Serve garnished with parsley.

Spicy fish and capsicum soup

Serves 4

You only need one mouthful to experience the warmth of this simple soup.

1 onion, peeled and finely diced

1 red chilli, seeded and finely chopped

2 teaspoons finely chopped fresh ginger

1 teaspoon cumin

1 teaspoon turmeric

1 tablespoon red curry paste

1 tablespoon apple juice concentrate

1 yellow capsicum, seeded and sliced

1 red capsicum, seeded and sliced

1 litre basic chicken stock (page 16) or Asian chicken stock (page 17)

500 g firm white fish fillets, cut into bite-sized pieces

2 teaspoons finely grated lemon rind

2 teaspoons finely chopped coriander

1 cup cooked warm white or brown rice to garnish

- In a shallow heavy-based pan, fat-free cook (see page 12) onion, chilli, ginger, cumin, turmeric, curry paste and apple juice concentrate until onion is soft and spices are fragrant.

- Add capsicums and stock and simmer until capsicum is tender.

- Add fish and simmer for a few minutes or until fish is just cooked.

- Add lemon rind and coriander.

- Serve garnished with a spoonful of rice.

St Patrick's Day soup
(Creamy spinach and tofu soup)

Serves 4–6

If you're looking for a deliciously different, vibrant green soup to serve on St Patrick's Day, this is it.

2 cups basic chicken stock
(page 16) or light vegetable stock
(page 26)

1 onion, peeled and chopped

2 sticks celery, chopped

500 g spinach, washed thoroughly

freshly ground black pepper

150 g silken tofu, well drained
and chopped

pinch nutmeg

finely chopped fresh parsley or
chives

- Combine all ingredients except tofu, nutmeg and herbs in a large soup pot. Bring to the boil, cover and simmer for 10 minutes or until spinach has just wilted and is still a vibrant green.

- Add tofu, nutmeg and herbs and purée until thick and creamy. Reheat, but do not boil, then serve.

Sweet potato and carrot soup

Serves 4–6

Sweet potatoes are sometimes referred to as 'the near-perfect food', not because they are sweet but because of their high nutritional value. They are high in vitamin A, potassium and calcium, as well as being loaded with fibre. Teamed here with sweet young carrots you could be forgiven for thinking this soup was heaven-sent.

500 g sweet potato, peeled

500 g sweet young carrots, chopped

200 g leek (white part only), thoroughly washed and chopped

2 cloves garlic, roasted

1 teaspoon cumin

1 teaspoon basil

5 litres light vegetable stock (page 26) or basic chicken stock (page 16)

low-fat yoghurt to garnish

green pesto (page 45) to garnish

- Place all ingredients except yoghurt and pesto in a large soup pot. Bring to the boil, cover and simmer until vegetables are soft.

- Remove from heat and purée until smooth and creamy.

- Serve garnished with yoghurt and pesto.

Sweet potato mulligatawny soup

Serves 4–6

Everyone has a favourite mulligatawny soup. It's one of those soup recipes that allows you to use all your left-over vegetables in the one pot and still turn out a delicious spicy brew. Mulligatawny is traditionally served with a big spoonful of rice in the centre. If you don't like the idea of rice, try a garnish of yoghurt or coconut milk.

1 tablespoon olive oil

1 teaspoon sesame oil

1 teaspoon crushed garlic

1 teaspoon finely chopped fresh ginger

1 tablespoon finely chopped fresh coriander root

1 onion, peeled and finely diced

1 tablespoon red curry paste

1 teaspoon cumin

½ teaspoon cinnamon

2 tablespoons tomato paste

500 g sweet potato, peeled

1 carrot, chopped

2 Granny Smith apples, peeled, cored and chopped

1.5 litres basic chicken stock (page 16) or light vegetable stock (page 26)

low-fat yoghurt or coconut milk to garnish

finely chopped fresh coriander to garnish

cooked brown or white rice for serving (optional)

- In a heavy-based pan, sauté oils, garlic, ginger, coriander root, onion, curry paste, cumin and cinnamon until onion begins to soften and brown.

- Add tomato paste, sweet potato, carrot, apples and stock. Bring to the boil, cover and simmer for 15 to 20 minutes or until sweet potato and apple are soft. Purée soup.

- Serve in individual bowls garnished with yoghurt or coconut milk and coriander or a spoonful of rice topped with coriander.

Sweet and sour pumpkin and coriander soup

Serves 4–6

Butternut pumpkin is unique in its flavour, colour and texture.

3 onions, peeled and diced

1 tablespoon finely chopped fresh ginger

2 teaspoons coriander

1 teaspoon cumin

1 teaspoon sweet chilli sauce

1 kg butternut pumpkin, peeled and chopped

3 cups light vegetable stock (page 26), basic chicken stock (page 16) or miso stock (page 23)

1 cup freshly squeezed orange juice

pinch salt

low-fat yoghurt to garnish

finely chopped fresh coriander to garnish

dry-roasted sesame seeds to garnish

- In a heavy-based pan, fat-free cook (see page 12) onions, ginger, coriander, cumin and sweet chilli sauce until onion begins to soften and brown.

- Add pumpkin, stock and orange juice and cook until pumpkin is soft. Purée soup.

- Add salt to taste.

- Serve garnished with swirls of yoghurt, topped with coriander and sesame seeds.

Thai pumpkin soup

Serves 4–6

Thai flavours are to die for! Try this Thai-flavoured pumpkin soup.

1 onion, peeled and diced

2 sticks celery, chopped

1 teaspoon finely chopped fresh ginger

3 teaspoons red curry paste

800 g pumpkin, peeled and chopped

200 g potato, peeled and chopped

1 litre Asian chicken stock (page 17) or basic chicken stock (page 16)

150 ml coconut milk

2 tablespoons finely chopped coriander

2 teaspoons finely chopped kaffir lime leaves

2 tablespoons toasted shredded coconut to garnish

2 tablespoons dry-roasted chopped peanuts to garnish

- In a heavy-based pan, fat-free cook (see page 12) onion, celery, ginger and curry paste until they begin to soften and brown.

- Add pumpkin, potato and stock. Bring to the boil, cover and simmer for 20 to 30 minutes or until vegetables are soft. Purée soup.

- Stir in coconut milk, coriander and lime leaves.

- Serve garnished with coconut and peanuts.

Thin chicken and asparagus soup

Serves 4–6

A light soup that makes staying in shape easy.

400 g chicken fillet (skin and fat removed), thinly sliced

1 onion, peeled and thinly sliced

2 sticks celery, thinly sliced

1 litre Asian chicken stock (page 17) or basic chicken stock (page 16)

½ cup white wine

2-cm piece lemon grass

2 sprigs coriander

300 g fresh asparagus spears, thinly diagonally sliced

1 small red chilli, seeded and very thinly sliced

2 teaspoons finely chopped extra coriander

2 spring onions, finely chopped

- In a heavy-based pan, fat-free cook (see page 12) chicken, onion and celery until chicken is cooked on all sides and onion and celery have softened.

- Add stock, wine, lemon grass, coriander and asparagus. Bring to the boil, cover and simmer until asparagus is just tender and a vibrant green.

- Remove lemon grass and coriander.

- Add chilli, extra coriander and spring onions and heat through before serving.

Tomato and oregano soup

Serves 4–6

In the middle of winter when ripe, robust tomatoes are hard to find, you can make this tasty tomato soup – with canned tomatoes – in next to no time.

1 onion, peeled and diced

1 teaspoon crushed garlic

2 sticks celery, chopped

2 x 425 g cans salt-free tomatoes and juice, puréed

2 tablespoons tomato paste

1 teaspoon dried basil

½ cup white wine

1–2 teaspoons finely chopped fresh oregano

freshly ground pepper

- In a heavy-based pan, fat-free cook (see page 12) onion, garlic and celery until they begin to soften and brown.

- Add all remaining ingredients except pepper. Bring to the boil, cover and simmer for 20 to 30 minutes.

- Add pepper to taste and serve.

Tomato and roasted eggplant soup

Serves 6–8

I've fallen in love with what some say is the ugliest vegetable in the vegie patch! I find myself looking for all sorts of excuses to use it in recipes. The roasted eggplant flavour in this recipe complements the tomatoes magnificently and helps create the yummiest of soups.

2 eggplants

2 onions, peeled and diced

1 tablespoon crushed garlic

2 x 810 g cans salt-free tomatoes and juice

2 cups basic chicken stock (page 16) or light vegetable stock (page 26)

½ cup white wine

1 teaspoon basil

⅛ teaspoon cayenne pepper

chopped chives to garnish

- Degorge eggplants (see page 12) then chargrill (see page 11) and roughly chop.

- Combine all other ingredients except chives in a large soup pot. Bring to the boil, cover and simmer for 20 to 30 minutes.

- Add eggplant and purée soup.

- Serve garnished with chives.

Tuscan vegetable soup

A little taste of Tuscany in your kitchen.

2 onions, peeled and diced

1 tablespoon crushed garlic

1 x 425 g can salt-free tomatoes and juice, puréed

1 teaspoon basil

½ cup tomato paste

1 cup red wine

200 g potato, peeled and cubed

200 g pumpkin, peeled and cubed

200 g carrot, sliced

200 g zucchini, sliced

100 g French beans, cut into 4-cm lengths

1 litre light vegetable stock (page 26) or basic chicken stock (page 16)

2 tablespoons finely chopped olives

freshly ground black pepper

finely chopped fresh flat-leaf parsley or basil to garnish

- In a heavy-based pan, fat-free cook (see page 12) onions and garlic until they soften and begin to brown.

- Add all remaining ingredients except olives, pepper and fresh herbs. Bring to the boil, cover and simmer for 20 to 30 minutes or until vegetables are soft.

- Add olives and warm through.

- Add pepper to taste.

- Serve garnished with parsley or basil.

Vichyssoise

This soup tastes delicious hot or cold. For a special occasion, add some cooked salmon and lots of fresh dill as a garnish.

400 g leek (white part only), thoroughly washed and chopped

500 g potato, peeled and chopped

1.5 litres basic chicken stock (page 16)

1 x 150 ml can low-fat evaporated milk or low-fat milk

pinch salt

freshly ground black pepper

finely chopped fresh chives to garnish

- In a heavy-based pan, fat-free cook (see page 12) leeks until soft. Be careful not to brown them.

- Add potato and stock. Bring to the boil, cover and simmer for 20 to 30 minutes or until potato is soft. Purée soup.

- Stir in the milk and reheat, but do not boil.

- Add salt and pepper to taste.

- Serve garnished with chives.

Vegetable laksa

Serves 6

Any vegetable can be used in this recipe in any combination. I like to use sweet snow peas, cabbage, yellow capsicum, broccoli and pumpkin. Be careful not to overcook the vegetables: for best results, ensure they are al dente and vibrant in colour.

200 g fresh hokkien noodles

100 g snow peas, cut into thin julienne strips

100 g carrot, cut into thin julienne strips

100 g yellow zucchini, cut into thin julienne strips

1–2 heads bok choy, washed and roughly chopped

100 g asparagus spears

1 red capsicum, seeded and cut into thin julienne strips

200 g sweet potato, peeled and cut into thin squares

1 litre dark vegetable stock (page 25) or miso stock (page 23), boiling

140 ml coconut milk

100 g bean shoots

fresh coriander to garnish

finely grated lemon rind to garnish

Laksa paste

2 teaspoons sesame oil

4 spring onions, finely diced

3 cloves garlic, peeled and crushed

3 teaspoons finely chopped fresh ginger

1 tablespoon finely chopped fresh lemon grass (approx. 1 stem, white part only)

8 macadamia nuts, finely diced

1 teaspoon turmeric

2 teaspoons cumin

1 teaspoon ground coriander

1–2 teaspoons sambal oelek or finely chopped red chilli

2 tablespoons fish sauce

3 tablespoons apple juice concentrate

- Pour boiling water over the noodles in a large bowl and allow them to soak for 2 to 3 minutes or until soft. Drain well.

- Blanch (see page 11) snow peas, carrot, zucchini, bok choy, asparagus and capsicum.

- Cook potato until tender, but not too soft.

- In a heavy-based pan, cook the first 10 ingredients of the laksa paste until onion softens and spices are fragrant. Add remaining ingredients and cook a further minute, stirring continuously.

- Add boiling stock and simmer for approximately 5 minutes.

- Stir in the coconut milk and heat through, but do not boil.

- Add vegetables and heat through.

- Place equal amounts of cooked noodles at the bottom of each soup bowl. Top with bean shoots.

- Ladle spoonfuls of soup over the noodles.

- Serve garnished with coriander and lemon rind.

White bean and vegetable soup

Serves 8

Simmer slowly so that all the flavours marry and settle. If you can, allow it to stand for a day or so: you won't believe how the flavours become even more harmonious . . . Just like a perfect marriage should be!

250 g dry white beans

2 leeks, thoroughly washed and chopped into 4-cm lengths

2 carrots, sliced

2 sticks celery, sliced

2 zucchini or 20 French beans, cut into 2-cm lengths

4 yellow squash, sliced

1 yellow capsicum, seeded and roughly chopped

4 bay leaves

1 tablespoon tomato paste

2 tablespoons low-salt soy sauce

2.5 litres basic chicken stock (page 16) or light vegetable stock (page 26)

1 cup chopped spinach

freshly ground black pepper

finely chopped fresh parsley to garnish

- Cook beans in plenty of simmering water until just tender, but not mushy. Drain well. The cooking liquid can be used as a stock, but it's not as flavoursome as a chicken, beef or vegetable stock.

- Combine all other ingredients except spinach, pepper and parsley in a large soup pot. Bring to the boil, cover and simmer for 20 to 30 minutes or until vegetables are soft.

- Add beans and cook a further 15 to 20 minutes.

- Remove bay leaves and discard.

- Add spinach and cook until spinach just wilts.

- Add pepper to taste.

- Serve garnished with parsley.

Yellow mellow soup

Serves 4–6

An unusual name for an unusual combination of yellow vegetables and spices that produces a golden Asian-style soup. If I'd called it squash and capsicum soup it would still taste the same, but I wonder if you'd have given it a second glance . . .

1 onion, peeled and chopped

1 teaspoon finely chopped fresh ginger

1 teaspoon vindaloo curry paste

½ teaspoon turmeric

1 teaspoon sesame oil

500 g yellow squash, chopped

200 g potato, peeled and chopped

2 yellow capsicums, seeded and chopped

1 litre basic chicken stock (page 16) or miso stock (page 23)

¼ cup coconut milk

finely chopped fresh chives or coriander to garnish

- In a heavy-based pan, fat-free cook (see page 12) onion, ginger, curry paste and turmeric until onion is soft.

- Add sesame oil, vegetables and stock. Bring to the boil, cover and simmer for 20 to 30 minutes or until vegetables are soft. Purée soup.

- Stir in the coconut milk.

- Serve garnished with chives or coriander.

Zucchini soup

Serves 4–6

An economical soup, especially if you grow your own zucchini or buy them cheaply when they're in season. For a simple change, leave out the nutmeg and parmesan cheese and garnish with some crumbled low-fat feta cheese instead.

1 small leek, thoroughly washed and chopped

1 tablespoon crushed garlic

1 kg zucchini, topped and tailed and chopped

400 g potato, peeled and chopped

1.25 litres basic chicken stock (page 16) or roasted chicken stock (page 18)

1 cup low-fat milk

pinch salt

freshly ground black pepper

nutmeg or parmesan cheese to garnish

- In a heavy-based pan, fat-free cook (see page 12) leek and garlic until soft. Be careful not to brown them.

- Add zucchini, potato and stock. Bring to the boil, cover and simmer for 20 to 30 minutes or until zucchini and potato are soft. Purée soup.

- Stir in the milk and reheat, but do not boil.

- Add salt and pepper to taste.

- Serve garnished with nutmeg or cheese or a little of both.

DAMPERS

Serve your soups with a damper or perhaps some oven-hot savoury muffins and you'll satisfy the appetites of the whole household.

Basil, olive and pepita damper

1 cup unbleached self-raising flour

1 cup unbleached wholemeal plain flour

2 teaspoons baking powder

1 cup chopped fresh basil leaves

20 green olives, stoned and chopped

2 tablespoons parmesan cheese

¼ cup pepitas (green pumpkin seeds)

2 tablespoons low-fat yoghurt

1 cup low-fat soymilk or low-fat milk

extra milk

extra pepitas

- Preheat oven to 180°C.

- Sift flours and baking powder into a bowl.

- Add basil, olives, cheese, pepitas, yoghurt and milk and mix to a sticky dough. Turn dough onto a lightly floured bench and knead.

- Shape dough into a long loaf and place on a baking tray lined with non-stick baking paper.

- Wipe top of loaf with a little extra milk and scatter extra pepitas over the top. With a sharp knife make two shallow cuts across the top.

- Bake for 25 to 30 minutes or until damper crust is brown and sounds hollow when tapped.

- Remove damper from oven, wrap in a tea towel and allow to cool slightly before slicing.

Beetroot, apple and walnut damper

1 cup unbleached self-raising flour

1 cup unbleached wholemeal plain flour

2 teaspoons baking powder

100 g raw beetroot, grated

1 Granny Smith apple, peeled, cored and finely diced

¼ cup finely chopped walnuts

1 teaspoon celery seeds

2 tablespoons low-fat yoghurt

1 cup low-fat soymilk or low-fat milk

extra milk

extra walnuts (optional)

- Preheat oven to 180°C.

- Sift flours and baking powder into a bowl.

- Add beetroot, apple, walnuts, celery seeds, yoghurt and milk and mix to a sticky dough. Turn dough onto a lightly floured bench and knead.

- Shape dough into a long loaf and place on a baking tray lined with non-stick baking paper.

- Wipe top of loaf with extra milk and, if using, scatter extra walnuts over the top. With a sharp knife make two shallow cuts across the top.

- Bake for 25 to 30 minutes or until damper crust is brown and sounds hollow when tapped.

- Remove damper from oven, wrap in a tea towel and allow to cool slightly before slicing.

Corn and cumin damper

1 cup unbleached self-raising flour

1 cup unbleached wholemeal plain flour

½ cup polenta

2 teaspoons baking powder

1 teaspoon cumin

2 teaspoons mustard seeds

1 x 130 g can corn kernels, well drained or ½ cup steam-cooked or dry-roasted fresh corn kernels

1 tablespoon parmesan cheese

1 teaspoon crushed garlic

1 cup finely chopped spring onion (green and white part)

2 tablespoons low-fat yoghurt

1 cup low-fat soymilk or low-fat milk

- Preheat oven to 180°C.

- Sift flours, polenta, baking powder and cumin into a bowl.

- Add mustard seeds, corn, cheese, garlic, spring onion, yoghurt and milk and mix to a sticky dough. Turn dough onto a lightly floured bench and knead.

- Shape dough into a long loaf and place on a baking tray lined with non-stick baking paper. With a sharp knife make two shallow cuts across the top.

- Bake for 25 to 30 minutes or until damper crust is brown and sounds hollow when tapped.

- Remove damper from oven, wrap in a tea towel and allow to cool slightly before slicing.

Green pesto and pine nut damper

2 cups unbleached self-raising flour

1 cup unbleached wholemeal plain flour

2 teaspoons baking powder

½ cup green pesto (page 45)

1–1¼ cups low-fat soymilk or low-fat milk

½ cup finely chopped pine nuts

- Preheat oven to 180°C.

- Sift flours and baking powder into a bowl.

- Stir in the pesto and milk and mix to a sticky dough. Turn dough onto a lightly floured bench and knead.

- Shape dough into a long loaf and place on a baking tray lined with non-stick baking paper.

- Scatter pine nuts over the top. With a sharp knife make two shallow cuts across the top.

- Bake for 25 to 30 minutes or until damper crust is brown and sounds hollow when tapped.

- Remove damper from oven, wrap in a tea towel and allow to cool slightly before slicing.

Mega-grain damper

1 tablespoon poppy seeds

2 tablespoons sesame seeds

2 tablespoons sunflower seeds

2 tablespoons pepitas (green
pumpkin seeds)

2 tablespoons cracked wheat

2 tablespoons soy flour

¼ cup polenta

2 cups unbleached self-raising
flour

2 teaspoons sesame oil

1¼ cups low-fat soymilk or
low-fat milk

- Preheat oven to 180°C.

- Place the first 7 ingredients in a bowl and sift over the flour.

- Add oil and milk and mix to a sticky dough. Turn dough onto a
  lightly floured bench and knead.

- Shape dough into a long loaf and place on a baking tray lined with
  non-stick baking paper. With a sharp knife make two shallow cuts
  across the top.

- Bake for 25 to 30 minutes or until damper crust is brown and
  sounds hollow when tapped.

- Remove damper from oven, wrap in a tea towel and allow to cool
  slightly before slicing.

Onion and cheese damper

1 cup unbleached self-raising flour

1 cup unbleached wholemeal plain flour

2 teaspoons baking powder

1 tablespoon chopped chives

1 tablespoon parmesan cheese

1 teaspoon finely chopped garlic

1 cup finely diced onion

2 tablespoons low-fat yoghurt

1 cup low-fat soymilk or low-fat milk

- Preheat oven to 180°C.

- Sift flours and baking powder into a bowl.

- Add chives, cheese, garlic, onion, yoghurt and milk and mix to a sticky dough. Turn dough onto a lightly floured bench and knead.

- Shape dough into a long loaf and place on a baking tray lined with non-stick baking paper. With a sharp knife make two shallow cuts across the top.

- Bake for 25 to 30 minutes or until damper crust is brown and sounds hollow when tapped.

- Remove damper from oven, wrap in a tea towel and allow to cool slightly before slicing.

Pumpkin and dill damper

1 cup unbleached self-raising flour

1 cup unbleached wholemeal plain flour

2 tablespoons soy flour

2 teaspoons baking powder

2 tablespoons finely chopped fresh dill

1 cup firmly packed grated pumpkin

3 tablespoons low-fat yoghurt

1 cup low-fat soymilk or low-fat milk

- Preheat oven to 180°C.

- Sift flours and baking powder into a bowl.

- Add dill, pumpkin, yoghurt and milk and mix to a sticky dough. Turn dough onto a lightly floured bench and knead.

- Shape dough into a long loaf and place on a baking tray lined with non-stick baking paper. With a sharp knife make two shallow cuts across the top.

- Bake for 25 to 30 minutes or until damper crust is brown and sounds hollow when tapped.

- Remove damper from oven, wrap in a tea towel and allow to cool slightly before slicing.

Pumpkin, polenta and lemon grass damper

1 cup unbleached self-raising flour

½ cup unbleached wholemeal plain flour

2 tablespoons soy flour

¼ cup polenta

2 teaspoons baking powder

2 tablespoons chopped lemon grass

1 tablespoon finely chopped coriander

1 cup firmly packed grated pumpkin or carrot

1 teaspoon finely chopped garlic

2 tablespoons low-fat yoghurt

1 cup low-fat soymilk or low-fat milk

¼ cup sesame seeds

- Preheat oven to 180°C.

- Sift flours, polenta and baking powder into a bowl.

- Add lemon grass, coriander, pumpkin, garlic, yoghurt and milk and mix to a sticky dough. Turn dough onto a lightly floured bench and knead.

- Shape dough into a long loaf and place on a baking tray lined with non-stick baking paper.

- Scatter sesame seeds over the top. With a sharp knife make two shallow cuts across the top.

- Bake for 25 to 30 minutes or until damper crust is brown and sounds hollow when tapped.

- Remove damper from oven, wrap in a tea towel and allow to cool slightly before slicing.

Sun-dried tomato and mung bean damper

1 cup unbleached wholemeal self-raising flour

1 cup unbleached wholemeal plain flour

2 teaspoons baking powder

1 cup fresh mung beans

½ cup well drained and chopped sun-dried tomatoes

lots of ground black pepper

1 teaspoon dried basil or 1 tablespoon finely chopped fresh basil

1–1¼ cups low-fat soymilk or low-fat milk

- Preheat oven to 180°C.

- Sift flours and baking powder into a bowl.

- Add mung beans, sun-dried tomatoes, pepper, basil and milk and mix to a sticky dough. Turn dough onto a lightly floured bench and knead.

- Shape dough into a long loaf and place on a baking tray lined with non-stick baking paper. With a sharp knife make two shallow cuts across the top.

- Bake for 25 to 30 minutes or until damper crust is brown and sounds hollow when tapped.

- Remove damper from oven, wrap in a tea towel and allow to cool slightly before slicing.

Sun-dried tomato, olive and onion damper

1 cup unbleached self-raising flour	½ cup finely diced onion
1 cup unbleached wholemeal plain flour	2 tablespoons low-fat yoghurt
2 teaspoons baking powder	1 cup low-fat soymilk or low-fat milk
½ cup well drained and chopped sun-dried tomatoes	8 extra black olives, stoned and chopped
12 black olives, stoned and chopped	1 tablespoon grated parmesan cheese

- Preheat oven to 180°C.

- Sift flours and baking powder into a bowl.

- Add sun-dried tomatoes, olives, onion, yoghurt and milk and mix to a sticky dough. Turn dough onto a lightly floured bench and knead.

- Shape dough into a long loaf and place on a baking tray lined with non-stick baking paper.

- Scatter olives and cheese over the top. With a sharp knife make two shallow cuts across the top.

- Bake for 25 to 30 minutes or until damper crust is brown and sounds hollow when tapped.

- Remove damper from oven, wrap in a tea towel and allow to cool slightly before slicing.

Index